Practical Debugging in C++

Ann R. Ford and Toby J. Teorey
University of Michigan

Prentice Hall
Upper Saddle River, NJ 07458

CIP data on file.

Vice President and Editorial Director, ECS: *Marcia Horton*
Senior Acquisitions Editor: *Petra J. Recter*
Editorial Assistant: *Karen Schultz*
Vice President and Director of Production and Manufacturing, ESM: *David W. Riccardi*
Executive Managing Editor: *Vince O'Brien*
Managing Editor: *David A. George*
Production Editor: *Lakshmi Balasubramanian*
Director of Creative Services: *Paul Belfanti*
Manager of Electronic Composition & Digital Content: *Jim Sullivan*
Electronic Composition: *William Johnson*
Creative Director: *Carole Anson*
Art Director: *Jayne Conte*
Art Editor: *Greg Dulles*
Cover Designer: *Joseph Sengotta*
Manufacturing Manager: *Trudy Pisciotti*
Manufacturing Buyer: *Lisa McDowell*
Marketing Manager: *Jennie Burger*

© 2002 by Prentice Hall, Inc.
Prentice-Hall, Inc.
Upper Saddle River, New Jersey 07458

The author and publisher of this book have used their best efforts in preparing this book. These efforts include the development, research, and testing of the theories to determine their effectiveness. The author and publisher make no warranty of any kind, expressed or implied, with regard to the documentation contained in this book.

Visual C++® is a registered trademark of the Microsoft Corporation, Redmond, WA.

Code Warrior® is a registered trademark of Metrowerks, Austin, TX.

Printed in the United States of America

10 9 8 7 6 5 4 3 2

ISBN 0-13-065394-2

Pearson Education Ltd., *London*
Pearson Education Australia Pty. Ltd., *Sydney*
Pearson Education Singapore, Pte. Ltd.
Pearson Education North Asia Ltd., *Hong Kong*
Pearson Education Canada, Inc., *Toronto*
Pearson Educacíon de Mexico, S.A. de C.V.
Pearson Education—Japan, *Tokyo*
Pearson Education Malaysia, Pte. Ltd.

To my son and daughter, Eric and Christan—A.R.F
To Eunice and Tom—T.J.T

Contents

Preface

This book is a tutorial on debugging techniques for both the beginning and intermediate programmer. For the beginning programmer it is meant to be a companion book to any introduction to programming in C++. Ideally this book is for students to take to their computer labs with them for quick reference when writing and debugging C++ programs. For the intermediate programmer, particularly those with some experience in other languages, this guide provides a quick up-to-speed primer in C++ debugging with a series of examples of common syntax and semantic errors and how they can be detected and corrected.

The motivation for this book came as a result of innumerable sessions in the computer lab with introductory programming classes at the University of Michigan. Unfortunately, many beginning programmers subscribe to the "programming by blind faith" method, writing the complete program, then hoping it will run correctly the first time without doing any intermediate testing, and then panicking when it crashes or generates bad data that cannot be explained. Each time they come to us with "What do I do now?" we go back to the program together to look over the basic logic, and then start inserting traces to check the intermediate results and localize the sources of error. We have come to the conclusion that students need a short, clear debugging guide as a valuable addition to their other programming tools, something they can easily carry with them and with which they can supplement their introductory programming textbooks.

Chapter 1 is a short motivational chapter that summarizes the common sources of errors in computer programs.

Chapter 2 describes the most common syntactic and semantic programming errors (with illustrative examples) and explains how to correct them.

Chapter 3 shows the student how to use output statements (cout) to trace variables in C++ programs, and how tracing can be easily inserted into his or her own programs. Several examples are given to illustrate how tracing can help find bugs—especially when a program runs without any runtime errors, but the results are incorrect. It also is useful to find errors quickly when the program crashes with an error message or just hangs up, leaving the programmer with no option but to kill the program and reboot the computer, over and over, until the bug is found.

Chapter 4 applies the basic principles of tracing to more advanced C++ constructs, such as strings, pointers, structs, and classes.

Chapter 5 illustrates how to use a debugger effectively as follow-on to the tracing method discussed in Chapters 3 and 4. Most compilers come with debuggers now, and students need to be able to use them at some point during their first course in programming. We strongly recommend learning to use both tracing and the debugger as alternative approaches.

The appendices give a summary of the most common bugs found in first C++ programs and a checklist of techniques for error detection and prevention. The examples in this book conform to the 1998 ISO/ANSI C++ standard.

Who should read this book?

Beginning programmers should benefit from this book because it is a quick read with many simple examples, both numeric and non-numeric. It should save them many frustrating hours of debugging time when they apply the tracing and system debugger techniques illustrated in Chapters 3 to 5. Furthermore, anyone using this book can easily read any chapter independently of the others. This should also appeal to the more experienced programmers who want to review their knowledge of debugging without wading through all the fundamentals. Instructors in introductory programming classes may want to recommend this book to their students, because it will make them much more self sufficient, and it will greatly reduce the time they need for individual counseling for their programs.

How to use this book

Beginning programmers should read Chapters 1 and 2 to get a quick overview of the basic types of errors programmers tend to make. Chapters 3 and 4 are self-contained discussions of how to use tracing in your programs with a minimum of effort. Chapter 5 is more advanced and may be used later, when you feel the need for more debugging options, especially for larger programs.

CHAPTER 1

Introduction

1.1 CHAPTER OBJECTIVES

- To motivate the programmer to learn and use debugging skills from the start
- To understand what types of errors occur in programs
- To learn what types of debugging tools and techniques are generally available to find and correct these different types of errors

1.2 MOTIVATION FOR DEBUGGING SKILLS

We all have read numerous stories of the results of poor programming, from banking errors that result in a loss (or gain) of funds for no apparent reason, to medical records mistakes, or spacecraft communication systems that go awry. In some cases serious injury or worse has been caused by public transportation failures or medical equipment failures due to computer software errors. These spectacular problems have led to the rise and importance of professional ethics and responsibility in the computing profession, to try to minimize and eventually remove the sources of errors.

These problems are often the results of errors or "bugs" that were introduced into the software code by the programmer and never detected nor corrected. In order to minimize the errors you get in programs, it is extremely important to learn the skills of good programming early and keep them constantly in mind. A very good reference for good programming design and implementation is the popular book *The Practice of Programming*, by Kernighan and Pike (see KePi99).

Good programming skills are learned through hard work and attention to detail. A well-designed program will eliminate many, but not all, errors. Program coding will often generate errors, even for a well-designed system, and the code will need to be closely checked at all stages of implementation. Compilers, which translate your source code into machine executable code, will check your syntax and generate error messages, so you can quickly find the errors and correct them.

After the syntax errors have been corrected, you are mostly on your own to find so-called "semantic" errors—that is, code that has correct syntax, but still has incorrect logic (meaning) and thus generates errors during program execution. Some of these errors are very hard to detect, so you need to develop special skills to find them. It is the main purpose of this book to give you the skills necessary to find and correct semantic errors. The two most important approaches to correcting semantic errors are tracing using C++ output statements and using the system interactive debugger. Examples of semantic errors that commonly occur in first programs include using "<" instead of "<=" to decide when to terminate a loop, accessing array elements that go beyond the original array definition, or simply forgetting to initialize your variables.

Many errors that occur during program execution may be due less to program logic than to data values that cause problems. A typical example of such an error occurs when the denominator becomes zero just before a division operation is attempted, and the system generates an error message like "program error: attempted to divide by zero." Another error message could occur when the result of a multiplication or other arithmetic operation generates a value that is too large (or too small) to be adequately represented by the numerical limits of your computer, thus generating a message "program error: numerical overflow (or underflow)." These types of errors can also be detected and corrected with the tracing techniques or use of the debugger that we recommend in this book. They can also be detected and dealt with automatically in object-oriented C++ using exception handling techniques, but this approach is beyond the scope of this book. For more detailed discussion, refer to a more advanced textbook in C++, such as Deitel and Deitel [DeDe01] or Savitch [Savi01].

Some errors are created by bad input data and are not necessarily the fault of the programmer. However, it is still the programmer's duty to include in his or her code ways to check for bad input data, to generate error messages when bad data is found, and in some cases, to terminate the program execution. This is often referred to as "error checking" code.

1.3   APPROACHES TO DEBUGGING

When semantic or other run-time errors occur, there are three basic approaches you can take to determine what the problem is and how to correct it:

1. Trace by hand

In this approach, you look at a program listing and trace each step of program execution by hand and try to recreate the results of the actual program execution. This is usually a good starting point for error correction, especially for small programs or simple functions. It forces you to think through the program logic in a methodical manner. For large programs, this process can be very time consuming, and you may then have to resort to computer-aided (program) tracing.

2. Program tracing

Program tracing (see Chapters 3 and 4) uses tracing (print) statements inserted into programs at key locations to track the changing of variable values so you can see how the program is progressing, step by step. Basic tracing can be done by inserting individual "cout" statements in C++ and using them to specify the location of the trace and current value of all variables. Extended tracing involves the use of flags and function calls to make the tracing easier to turn on and off and to minimize the amount of code that has to be written and inserted into the program.

3. System interactive debugger

Most programming language environments in use today include a debugger (see Chapter 5), a software package that allows you to run your program in a step-by-step mode, automatically keeping track of all variables in the program as it executes one step (statement) at a time. You can also set breakpoints which allow the program to run free of tracing overhead to a certain location, and then stop to display all the program variables and their values.

All of these debugging techniques are valuable to understand and use. We recommend that you start with tracing by hand because it forces you to make sure you fully understand the program requirements and what your program logic is doing. When this is no longer giving you any insight about where to locate runtime errors, we recommend the extensive use of program tracing with inserted output (cout) statements. In most programs, this method will find all semantic and other run-time errors and should be sufficient. In some cases, however, you may want to use the system interactive debugger. The choice between program tracing and using the system debugger is often one of personal style, but it is important to know how to use both, so that your choice is an informed one. Now, on with the details of debugging!

CHAPTER 2

Common Syntax and Semantic Errors

2.1 CHAPTER OBJECTIVES

- To understand the fundamental characteristics of syntax and semantic errors
- To be able to identify specific common syntax and semantic errors frequently encountered by beginning programmers
- To be able to interpret a syntax warning
- To be able to apply appropriate techniques to correct these common errors

2.2 SYNTAX ERRORS

A *syntax error* is a violation of the syntax, or grammatical rules, of a natural language or a programming language. The following sentence contains an error of English syntax:

```
I is going to the concert tonight.
```

If we write or say this sentence, other English speakers will know that we have used incorrect grammar, however they will still understand what we *mean*. Programming languages are not so forgiving, however. If we write a line of C++ code containing a syntax error, the compiler does *not* know what we mean. A syntax error is called a *fatal compilation error*, because the compiler cannot translate a C++ program into executable code if even one syntax error is present.

2.2.1   Syntax Errors: Summary of Important Points

- *How are they detected?* The compiler detects them when you try to compile your program.
- *Why do they occur?* The syntax rules of C++ have been violated.
- *Is there object-code generated?* No, so you cannot run the program.
- Solution: Find the line(s) containing the syntax error(s) using the compiler's flagged lines and error messages; using your textbook or other C++ reference as a guide, correct them.
- Remember, frequently, a syntax error occurs not in the line flagged by your compiler, but in some line *above* that line; it is often the previous line, but not necessarily.

2.2.2   Examples: Common Syntax Errors

Some syntax errors are very common, especially for beginning programmers, and the examples that follow should help you identify and correct many syntax errors in whatever program you are currently working on. The syntax diagrams in your C++ textbook or a C++ reference book should be your ultimate guide in correcting these types of errors.

Different compilers report syntax errors in different formats. For these examples, we will assume that the compiler displays errors for a C++ program named "myprog.cpp" in the following way:

```
Syntax Error: <description of error>
Line <line number here> of program myprog.cpp
```

The first line indicates that a syntax error message is being displayed and then gives a brief description of what the compiler thinks the error is. The second line will give the line number on which the compiler has identified the error.

Compilers that provide a graphical user interface (GUI) using windows and various graphical items to display information for you may display all such error messages in one window (which we will assume for our discussion here), or they may simply list the program with erroneous lines highlighted or pointed to by an arrow or other graphic, with written error messages shown off to the side. In any event, error messages displayed by different compilers generally are very similar.

An important note about compilers: Modern compilers typically are very accurate in identifying syntax errors and will help you enormously in correcting your code. However, compilers often present two difficult problems for new programmers: (1) they frequently can miss reporting an actual error on one line but get "thrown off track," then report errors on subsequent lines that are not truly errors; the compiler may then also display error messages which are incorrect; and (2) after encountering one true syntax error, compilers often generate many incorrect syntax error messages; again, the compiler has been "thrown off track" by a particular error. Why does this occur? Basically, because a compiler is a very complex and sophisticated language-processing program, and no computer program can analyze any language as well as a human being can at this point in time.

What, then, is your best strategy for eliminating syntax errors?

- Display the current list of syntax errors (print it if you like)
- Start at the first error listed, try to correct it, and then re-compile your program; sometimes many errors will drop out after one error is fixed
- If you are having trouble with a particular error listed for a specific line, yet you are 100% sure that line is correct, then search for a syntax error in the lines ABOVE that line, starting with the line immediately preceeding the line under consideration, and working backwards; usually the actual error will be found in a line close to the line flagged, though not always
- Repeat this process until all errors are eliminated

Specific examples follow.

Missing Semicolon   In the C++ code that follows, three declarations are given. Line numbers (chosen in all examples arbitrarily) are shown to the left of each line.

```
5      int num;
6      float value
7      double bigNum;
```

A C++ compiler would generate an error something like the following:

```
Syntax Error: semi-colon expected
Line 6 of program myprog.cpp
```

To fix this error, simply add a semicolon after the identifier value, as in

```
6      float value;
```

Undeclared Variable Name - version 1   If the preceding code were compiled and included an assignment statement, as in

```
5      int num;
6      float value
7      double bigNum;
8      bigNum = num + value;
```

we would see the following additional error message:

```
Syntax Error: undeclared identifier "bigNum"
Line 8 of program myprog.cpp
```

This is a situation in which there is actually no syntax error on the line flagged, and the real error occurs on a line above it. Line 8 is totally correct. If we correct the problem in line 6, the error reported for line 8 will drop out the next time we compile the program.

Undeclared Variable Name - version 2 What about the following?

```
5     int num;
6     float value;
7     double bigNum;
8     bignum = num + value;
```

We would see the error message

```
Syntax Error: undeclared identifier "bignum"
Line 8 of program myprog.cpp
```

This is a different problem; in this case, an error actually exists on line 8. The lowercase n in bignum must be changed to an uppercase N, or else the variable name does not match its declaration. Remember, in C++ declarations, lowercase letters are different from uppercase letters.

Undeclared Variable Name - version 3 **Missing Reference to Namespace**
Consider the following program:

```
1     #include <iostream>
2     int main ( )
3     {
4          cout << "Hello World!!!";
5          return 0;
6     }
```

A compiler will generate an error message like this:

```
Syntax Error: undeclared identifer "cout"
Line 4 of program myprog.cpp
```

The problem is that cout is defined in a namespace named std. To correct this error, we need only add the following line, right after line 1 in the preceding program:

```
using namespace std;
```

Unmatched Parentheses   Given the code

```
5    result = (firstVal - secondVal / factor;
```

the compiler would generate an error message like

```
Syntax Error: ')' expected
Line 5 of program myprog.cpp
```

We could correct this error with

```
5    result = (firstVal - secondVal) / factor;
```

Note that similar syntax errors can occur with unmatched braces, { and }.

Unterminated Strings   It is easy to forget the last double quote in a string, as in

```
21   const string ERROR_MESSAGE = "bad data entered!;
```

or

```
45   cout << "Execution Terminated << endl;
```

Both will provoke the compiler to print something similar to

```
Syntax Error: illegal string constant
```

Both can be fixed by adding the terminating double quote to the string:

```
21   const string ERROR_MESSAGE = "bad data entered!";
```

or

```
45   cout << "Execution Terminated" << endl;
```

Left-Hand Side of Assignment does not Contain an L-Value   Look at the following statements, where the intent of the assignment statement in line 7 is to calculate x * y and store the result in product:

```
6    double x = 2.0, y = 3.1415, product;
7    x * y = product;
```

Many C++ compilers will print an error message like

```
Syntax Error: not an l-value
Line 7 of program myprog.cpp
```

But what does this mean? An "l-value" roughly refers to a value that specifies the address of a location in memory where something can be stored. We can think of it as the Left side of an assignment, and what we know about the syntax of this statement is that the left-hand side must contain the name of a *variable*. Nothing else is valid in this position. Therefore, we correct this error using

```
7    product = x * y;
```

Value-Returning Function has no Return Statement   A function declared with a return type must contain a return statement. Consider the following function, which is supposed to round its float parameter up or down appropriately:

```
int RoundFloat (float floatToRound)
{
      int roundedValue;
      roundedValue = int (floatToRound + 0.5);
}
```

This function calculates a correct result in the local variable roundedValue, but it never returns this result. Some compilers will merely generate a warning message for this function (to be discussed later in this chapter), others will generate a syntax error. In any event, the error can be corrected by adding a return statement, as in

```
int RoundFloat (float floatToRound)
{
      int roundedValue;
      roundedValue = int (floatToRound + 0.5);
      return (roundedValue);

}
```

Can't Convert int* to int** (and similar errors) Many times we need to pass an array to a function. Let's suppose we have the following declarations:

```
const int NUM_SCORES = 100;
typedef int ScoreList [NUM_SCORES];
void ProcessScores (ScoreList inputScores [NUM_SCORES]);
ScoreList scores;
```

Now let's assume we call the function ProcessScores and pass the array the variable scores like this:

```
10   ProcessScores (scores);
```

A compiler will generate an error message something like

```
Syntax Error: can't convert int* to int**
Line 10 of program myprog.cpp
```

What is wrong here? The data type of the argument `scores` and the data type of the corresponding parameter `inputScores` do *not* match. Array `scores` is a one-dimensional array of `int`. In the prototype we wrote earlier, `inputScores` is a two-dimensional array of `int`. The corrected version of the prototype for the function is

```
void ProcessScores (ScoreList inputScores);
```

Remember, the data types of arguments and parameters must generally match in three places—a function's prototype, its heading, and calls to that function. C++ does perform some type conversions automatically, but as part of defensive programming and good style, it is generally not wise to use data types that do not match.

Illegal Function Overloading   This is another common error message generated when the data types of arguments and parameters in a function's prototype, its heading, and calls to that function, do not all match. As discussed in the previous example, it is typically best to utilize matching data types in all of these three program elements. Note that this error message may be generated when you are trying to call a a C++ *library function*, as well as when you try to call functions you have written yourself.

2.3   SYNTAX WARNINGS

From the discussion thus far, you know that a syntax error is a *fatal compilation error*—that is, the compiler cannot translate your program into executable code. Compilers also can generate syntax *warning* messages, which are not fatal errors, and are often very helpful in the debugging process. A syntax warning is displayed when the compiler has found that the syntax of some part of your code is valid, but it is potentially erroneous anyway. Compiler writers, being programmers themselves, are familiar with common programming errors and usually build some error checking of this type into the compiler. Let's look at a few examples.

2.3.1   Syntax Warnings: Summary of Important Points

- *How are they detected?* The compiler detects them when you compile your program.
- *Why do they occur?* The syntax rules of C++ have *not* been violated, but the compiler writers have built in special error checking for certain common programming errors, and the compiler has found a possible error of this type.

- *Is there object-code generated?* Yes, so you can run the program.
- *Solution*: Find the line(s) containing the syntax warning(s), and check them very carefully to see if you think they contain true errors.
- Remember, a syntax warning should *always* be taken seriously, because there is probably a real error in your code if the compiler issues a warning message.

2.3.2   Examples: Common Syntax Warnings

Using "=" when "==" is Intended   Given the if statement

```
20    if (num = 100)
21        cout << "num equals 100";
22    else
23        cout << "num is not 100";
```

many compilers would display something like the following warning message:

```
Syntax Warning: assignment operator used in if expression
Line 20 of program myprog.cpp
```

What is the problem with this code? You may have noticed that the equal sign used in the if expression is actually an assignment operator, not the relational operator, which tests for equality. In this code, num is set to 100 because of the assignment, and the expression num = 100 is *always* true, because the value of the expression is actually 100. The corrected code for this example would be

```
20    if (num == 100)
```

Loop has no Body   Consider the following for loop, which is supposed to print out the numbers between 1 and 10, along with their squares:

```
9     int lcv;
10    for (lcv = 1; lcv <= 10; lcv++);
11    cout << lcv << " " << lcv * lcv
12        << endl;
```

This loop, if run, would print only

```
11        121
```

When we try to compile this loop, a good compiler would generate the following warning message:

```
Syntax Warning: for loop has no body
Line 10 of program myprog.cpp
```

We would correct this code by removing the erroneous semicolon, as follows:

```
10     for (int lcv = 1; lcv <= 10; lcv++)
```

Uninitialized Variable   Consider the following code, which is supposed to read characters until the user hits `return`:

```
10     char ch;
11     while (ch != '\n')
12         cin >> ch;
```

When we try to compile this version, many compilers would generate the following warning message:

```
Syntax Warning: variable "ch" is uninitialized
Line 11 of program myprog.cpp
```

In this code, the variable `ch` is tested for a value when it has not received a value yet. This code, as it is, will not execute correctly. We can fix this problem using a priming read, as follows:

```
10     char ch;
11     cin >> ch;
12     while (ch != '\n')
13         cin >> ch;
```

All of the errors discussed here which generate warning messages are what we call *semantic* errors, to be discussed in the next section.

To illustrate what we have looked at so far in this chapter, Figure 2.1 shows the syntax errors and warnings window generated by the Metrowerks CodeWarrior Professional Release 5 compiler for a specific program. Looking at this figure, notice in particular how errors and warnings are flagged with different graphics elements. Figure 2.2 shows the window generated by the Microsoft Visual C++ 6 compiler for the same program. Notice how the two compilers produce similar, but not identical, error reports. Other compilers will also produce similar error and warning messages.

Figure 2.1

Example Program in Metrowerks CodeWarrior Syntax Errors and Warnings Window

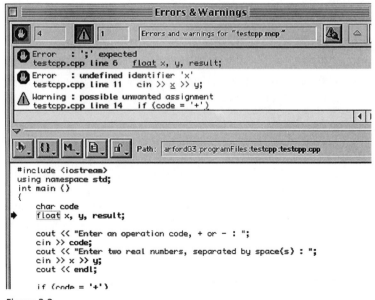

Figure 2.2

Example Program in Microsoft Visual C++ Syntax Errors and Warnings Window

2.4 SEMANTIC ERRORS

A *semantic error* is a violation of the rules of *meaning* of a natural language or a programming language. The following sentence contains an error of English semantics:

```
My refrigerator just drove a car to Chicago.
```

If we write or say this sentence, other English speakers may begin to wonder about our sanity, but they will nevertheless know that our syntax is perfectly correct! Since a compiler only checks for correct use of syntax, it is not able to evaluate whether or not we have written code whose *meaning* is correct. Semantic errors are much harder to detect and correct than syntax errors, and they are also more common.

When there are semantic errors in a C++ program, the compiler *does* translate the program into executable code. Most of the time, semantic errors do NOT generate compiler warnings. When the program is run, however, it does not work correctly.

2.4.1 Summary of Important Points

- *How are they detected?* Semantic errors usually are detected by the programmer or user of the program, often while reading output and finding it is incorrect.
- *Why do they occur?* The syntax rules of C++ have been correctly followed, but the meaning of the code is incorrect (e.g., faulty algorithms, algorithms not translated into C++ correctly, values calculated or input erroneously, flow of control is wrong, etc.).
- *Is there object-code generated?* Yes, so you can run the program.
- Solution: Find the line(s) containing the semantic error(s), using extra print statements, hand tracing, or an interactive debugger if needed, and correct them.
- Remember, semantic errors are undoubtedly the most common type of error, and they are the hardest to find and correct, so prevention in the form of good design and defensive programming are often your best tools.

2.4.2 Examples: Common Semantic Errors

Infinite Loop An infinite loop, which repeats indefinitely, is often created when a programmer writes a loop in which the expression tested never becomes false. For example, consider the following code, which is intended to read a lower case 'y' or 'n' from the user:

```
char response;
cout << "Please enter (y)es or (n)o -> ";
cin >> response;
while ((response != 'y') || (response != 'n'))
{
    cout << "Please try again. Enter (y)es or (n)o -> ";
    cin >> response;
}
```

The expression

```
(response != 'y') || response != 'n')
```

is always true, regardless of what input is entered by the user. If the user enters a 'y', then the first part of the expression is false, but the second part of the expression is true. Thus, the entire expression is true because of the OR operation. Because of this property, the loop is infinite. The following expression is the corrected version, which merely substitutes AND for OR and is false when the user enters either a 'y' or an 'n', allowing the loop to exit:

```
(response != 'y') && (response != 'n')
```

Misunderstanding of Operator Precedence   Misunderstanding of the operator precedence rules often can lead to expressions that evaluate data incorrectly. Consider the following code, which is intended to calculate the miles per gallon achieved by a car:

```
float startMileage,
      endMileage,
      gallonsUsed,
      milesPerGallon;
cout << "Please enter the starting mileage, the ending"
     << " mileage, and the number of gallons used by the"
     << " car -> ";
cin >> startMileage >> endMileage >> gallonsUsed;
milesPerGallon = endMileage - startMileage / gallonsUsed;
```

Since division has higher precedence than subtraction, the final assignment statement evaluates incorrectly. The corrected version is as follows:

```
milesPerGallon = (endMileage - startMileage) / gallonsUsed;
```

Programmers often make liberal use of parentheses to prevent this kind of error in the first place, as part of defensive programming.

Dangling Else   The "dangling else" is a very common and subtle error in the flow of control of a nested `if` statement. Remember, compilers ignore indentation, and pair an *else* clause with the most recent unmatched *then* clause. The following code is intended to print out the word "both" if the `bool` variables `relative` and `myFriend` are both true, and print out "neither" if both are false.

```
if (relative)
    if (myFriend)
        cout << "both";
else
    cout << "neither";
```

When this code is run, it prints "both" correctly when both `bool` variables are true. However, if both variables are false, it prints nothing. Further, when `relative` is true, but `myFriend` is false, it prints "neither!" There are many ways to fix or rewrite this code, but let's consider one very common correction technique here. The following code forces the compiler to pair the `else` with the first `if`, instead of with the second `if`, and therefore works correctly:

```
if (relative)

{
    if (myFriend)
        cout << "both";
}
else
    cout << "neither";
```

Off-By-One Error   The off-by-one error generally describes a loop that iterates one fewer or one more time than is correct. Consider the following code, which is supposed to read in 50 values from the user, and keep a running total:

```
const int NUM_VALUES = 50;
int lcv,
    someValue,
    total = 0;
for (lcv = 1; lcv < NUM_VALUES; lcv++)
{
    cout << "Enter an integer ->";
    cin >> someValue;
    total = total + someValue;
}
```

What happens when this code is executed? The user is prompted 49 times, and

49 values are read in and summed. The following small change in the `for` loop heading fixes this problem:

```
for (lcv = 1; lcv <= NUM_VALUES; lcv++)
```

Or, alternatively, we can write

```
for (lcv = 0; lcv < NUM_VALUES; lcv++)
```

Code inside a Loop that does not Belong There   The following code, adapted from the previous example, is intended to read in a series of 50 numbers entered by the user, calculate the running total, and print out both the final total and the average value of all the numbers:

```
const int NUM_VALUES = 50;
int lcv,
    someValue,
    total = 0,
    average;
for (lcv = 1; lcv <= NUM_VALUES; lcv++)
{
    cout << "Enter an integer ->";
    cin >> someValue;
    total = total + someValue;
    average = total / NUM_VALUES;
    cout << "Total is: " << total << endl;
    cout << "Average is: " << average;
}
```

When this code is executed, it produces a disturbing result! The output is very long, because the total and average are both printed out 50 times. Moreover, they are correct only the last time they are printed. What is wrong? The last three lines inside the loop do not belong there, they must be placed outside the loop and after it for the code to work correctly. The corrected version of this code is as follows:

```
for (lcv = 1; lcv <= NUM_VALUES; lcv++)
{
    cout << "Enter an integer ->";
    cin >> someValue;
    total = total + someValue;
}
average = total / NUM_VALUES;
cout << "Total is: " << total << endl;
cout << "Average is: " << average;
```

Not Using a Compound Statement When One is Required   The following code is intended to read in a text file and echoprint its contents (for this example, assume that `infile` is the file variable name and the file has just been opened successfully):

```
char ch;
infile.get (ch);
while (infile)          // while input stream has not failed
    cout << ch;         // echoprint the current character
    infile.get (ch);    // read the next character
```

The programmer has indented this code to show that both the `cout` and the `get` calls are inside the loop. However, the compiler interprets it differently. When executed, this code reads one character from the file (assuming the file does contain at least one character) and then enters an infinite loop, printing that same character over and over indefinitely. The following code contains the addition of a compound statement, and thus is correct:

```
infile.get (ch);
while (infile)          // while input stream has not failed
{
    cout << ch;         // echoprint the current character
    infile.get (ch);    // read the next character
}
```

Array Index Bounds Error   The following code is intended to read in seven temperature values, one for each day of the week, and load them into a seven-element array.

```
const int NUM_DAYS = 7;
int temperatures[NUM_DAYS];
int count;
for (count = 1; count <= NUM_DAYS; count++)
{
    cout << "Enter a temperature: ";
    cin >> temperatures [count];
}
```

Let's say that we execute this code as it is written. Many problems may result, because the code contains a fundamental error—the array's correct indices range from 0 through 6, while the array indices used in the `for` loop range from 1 through 7. The array element `temperatures[0]` is never used. The attempt to access an array element with `temperatures[7]` is wrong, because `temperatures[7]` does not exist.

The results of reading in the array with this loop and then attempting to use the array later in the same program are somewhat unpredictable and are partly dependent on what indices are used later on. The program may even crash (a runtime error). We may find that an error message such as "Bus Error" or "Segmentation Fault" is printed at the time of the crash. Alternatively, the program may keep running, and the value of the count may be overwritten by whatever value the user types in for the last array element, which causes other unpredictable behavior. The fundamental problem is that when invalid array indices are used, a C++ program will access memory locations that are not valid portions of the array. C++ does not prevent such array index errors by performing what is called "bounds checking." To avoid this problem, you must be very careful to write your code so that only valid indices are used. We can correct the code above by using this conventional `for` loop control for such an array:

```
for (count = 0; count < NUM_DAYS; count++)
```

A *Final Note*

This concludes our discussion of syntax errors and warnings, and semantic errors. While working on your programming assignments on a computer, you may wish to keep this book with you as a helpful guide in determining what exactly the compiler is trying to tell you when you see one of its sometimes obscure error messages. In addition, by studying the examples of all of the common errors described in this chapter, you may be able to prevent many of them from occurring in the first place, as you will have the knowledge and the tools to avoid them altogether.

C H A P T E R   3

Tracing Techniques for Debugging

3.1 CHAPTER OBJECTIVES

- To understand the principles of tracing as an effective debugging tool
- To be able to insert tracing code in your program to find run-time errors
- To learn how to enhance tracing with the use of an on/off flag, and to use calls to a tracing function that displays variable values
- To learn where to insert trace statements in your program and what variables to display

3.2 BASIC TRACING

Tracing using extra print statements probably is the single most important method for debugging computer programs. We will look at several simple examples of how tracing is done and how it can be of tremendous benefit to you when the computer crashes or hangs up and you don't have any idea where the error occurred, or when the program runs to completion without any crash or error message, but the output is incorrect. In both cases, you may or may not have a clue as to where the error is occurring, and unlike syntax errors that the compiler catches, you may not have any system messages to help in locating the problem.

Tracing is a method of inserting print statements into your program at key locations to print out (or just display on your screen) the current status (current value) of certain variables in your program so you can see how those values are changing during the execution of the program. You can follow the execution step by step if you wish by putting in print statements after every line of source code. However, this would not be an efficient use of time and energy—your trace can be done better with a careful selection of where to insert the print statements.

Let's look at a simple example of a numeric programming problem, taking a series of integers as input and performing some basic computations on those numbers, such as finding the minimum value, finding the maximum value, finding the sum of all the positive numbers, finding the sum of all the negative numbers, and finding the mean (average) value of all the positive and negative numbers, separately. The program is terminated when a value outside the legal range of values (from −1000 to +1000) is input. The program is shown in Fig. 3.1. As you can see, it is a simple main function in C++ with variable declarations and initialization; basic control statements such as if, else, and while; and some summary output.

Note that the example program has the same line numbers in all the examples in Figs. 3.1 to 3.10. Tracing code is shown as inserted lines with fractional line numbers.

```
/*Debugging Example This is a program to illustrate the basic debug-
ging procedure for beginning programmers. The main idea is to set up
tracing of the current values of major variables and see how well the
program is progressing. The goal of the program is to compute the
minimum and maximum values of all the numbers, then compute the sum
of the positive and negative values, separately, and find the mean of
the positive (including zero) and negative values separately. The
legal values are restricted to be between -1000 and +1000 inclusive-
ly*/
1 #include <iostream>
2 using namespace std;
3 int main()
4 {
5     const int MIN_VALUE = -1000;
6     const int MAX_VALUE = 1000;
7     int new_value;
8     int highest_value = MIN_VALUE-1;
9     int lowest_value = MAX_VALUE+1;
10    int count_pos_values = 0;
11    int count_neg_values = 0;
12    int sum_pos_values = 0;
13    int sum_neg_values = 0;
14    float mean_pos_values = 0.;
```

Figure 3.1

Example program without tracing

```
16
17   cout << "Please input a new value: ";
18   cin >> new_value;
19
20   while (new_value >= MIN_VALUE && new_value <= MAX_VALUE)
21   {
22        if (new_value > highest_value)
23            highest_value = new_value;
24
25        if (new_value < lowest_value)
26            lowest_value = new_value;
27
28        if (new_value >= 0 )
29        {
30            count_pos_values++;
31            sum_pos_values += new_value;
32        }
33
34        else
35        {
36            count_neg_values++;
37            sum_neg_values += new_value;
38        }
39
40        cout << "Please input a new value: ";
41        cin >> new_value;
42   }
43
44   mean_pos_values = float(sum_pos_values)/float(count_pos_values);
45   mean_neg_values = float(sum_neg_values)/float(count_neg_values);
46
47   //program output statement
48   cout << endl << "Final output of the program." << endl
49           << "Highest value is:" << highest_value
50           << " Lowest value is:" << lowest_value << endl
51           << "Sum of positives is:" << sum_pos_values
52           << " Sum of negatives is:" << sum_neg_values << endl
53           << "Mean of positives is:" << mean_pos_values
54           << " Mean of negatives is:" << mean_neg_values
                 << endl << endl;
55
56   return 0;
57 }              //end of main
```

Figure 3.1 (Continued)

Fig. 3.2 shows the same program with three trace statements added. The set of input values (integer numbers) is shown with a `cout` statement (Lines 17 and 40) that prompts the user for the next value, and a `cin` statement (Lines 18 and 41) that allows the next value to be input from the keyboard. For this example, we assume that there are six numeric values, input one at a time for each prompt: 917, −236, 14, −789, 1, and −67.

```
/*Debugging Example - This is the same program as in Fig. 3.1, but
now includes basic tracing statements */
1 #include <iostream>
2 using namespace std;
3 int main()
4 {
5       const int MIN_VALUE = -1000;
6       const int MAX_VALUE = 1000;
7       int new_value;
8       int highest_value = MIN_VALUE-1;
9       int lowest_value = MAX_VALUE+1;
10      int count_pos_values = 0;
11      int count_neg_values = 0;
12      int sum_pos_values = 0;
13      int sum_neg_values = 0;
14      float mean_pos_values = 0.;
15      float mean_neg_values = 0.;
16
17      cout << "Please input a new value: ";
18      cin >> new_value;
19
19.01     //debug trace statement
19.02     cout << endl << "Location 1:" << endl
19.03           << "New value read in is: " << new_value << endl
19.04           << "Highest value is:" << highest_value
19.05           << " Lowest value is:" << lowest_value << endl
19.06           << "Count of positives is:" << count_pos_values
19.07           << " Count of negatives is:" << count_neg_values
                 << endl
19.08           << "Sum of positives is:" << sum_pos_values
19.09           << " Sum of negatives is:" << sum_neg_values << endl
                 << endl;
19.10
20      while (new_value >= MIN_VALUE && new_value <= MAX_VALUE)
21      {
22          if (new_value > highest_value)
```

Figure 3.2

Example program with basic trace statements

```
23              highest_value = new_value;
24
25         if (new_value < lowest_value)
26              lowest_value = new_value;
27
28         if (new_value >= 0 )
29         {
30              count_pos_values++;
31              sum_pos_values += new_value;
32         }
33
34         else
35         {
36              count_neg_values++;
37              sum_neg_values += new_value;
38         }
39
39.01          //debug trace statement
39.02          cout << endl << "Location 2:" << endl
39.03               << "New value read in is: " << new_value << endl
39.04               << "Highest value is:" << highest_value
39.05               << " Lowest value is:" << lowest_value << endl
39.06               << "Count of positives is:" << count_pos_values
39.07               << " Count of negatives is:" << count_neg_values
                    << endl
39.08               << "Sum of positives is:" << sum_pos_values
39.09               << " Sum of negatives is:" << sum_neg_values
                    << endl << endl;
39.10
40         cout << "Please input a new value: ";
41         cin >> new_value;
42    }
43
43.01          //debug trace statement
43.02          cout << endl << "Location 3:" << endl
43.03               << "New value read in is: " << new_value << endl
43.04               << "Highest value is:" << highest_value
43.05               << " Lowest value is:" << lowest_value << endl
43.06               << "Count of positives is:" << count_pos_values
43.07               << " Count of negatives is:" << count_neg_values << endl
43.08               << "Sum of positives is:" << sum_pos_values
43.09               << " Sum of negatives is:" << sum_neg_values << endl
                    << endl;
43.10
```

Figure 3.2 (Continued)

```
44    mean_pos_values = float(sum_pos_values)/float(count_pos_values);
45    mean_neg_values = float(sum_neg_values)/float(count_neg_values);
46
47    //program output statement
48    cout << endl << "Final output of the program." << endl
49          << "Highest value is:" << highest_value
50          << " Lowest value is:" << lowest_value << endl
51          << "Sum of positives is:" << sum_pos_values
52          << " Sum of negatives is:" << sum_neg_values << endl
53          << "Mean of positives is:" << mean_pos_values
54          << " Mean of negatives is:" << mean_neg_values << endl
              << endl;
55
56    return 0;
57 }                  //end of main
```

Figure 3.2 (Continued)

Note that the program has three trace (cout) statements—after lines 19, 39, and 43. These are not part of the original program, having been inserted after the program was written. They will not be part of the final program either, and they should be deleted after the program has been debugged.

The program output, including the trace statement output, is shown in Fig. 3.3. Note that the first line of the program output is the prompt to the user, followed by the latest input value. This is followed by a blank line and a group of six lines representing the first trace statement output.

The first line of the trace output is a location number. This is important because it tells you where in the program this trace is originating. In our example, Location 1 is just after the first input value is obtained and allows you

```
Program output:
Please input a new value: 917
Location 1:
New value read in is: 917
Highest value is:-1001 Lowest value is:1001
Count of positives is:0 Count of negatives is:0
Sum of positives is:0 Sum of negatives is:0
Location 2:
New value read in is: 917
Highest value is:917 Lowest value is:917
Count of positives is:1 Count of negatives is:0
Sum of positives is:917 Sum of negatives is:0
Please input a new value:-236
```

Figure 3.3

Correct output from example program with tracing

```
Location 2:
New value read in is:-236
Highest value is:917 Lowest value is:-236
Count of positives is:1 Count of negatives is:1
Sum of positives is:917 Sum of negatives is:-236
Please input a new value: 14
Location 2:
New value read in is: 14
Highest value is:917 Lowest value is:-236
Count of positives is:2 Count of negatives is:1
Sum of positives is:931 Sum of negatives is:-236
Please input a new value:-789
Location 2:
New value read in is:-789
Highest value is:917 Lowest value is:-789
Count of positives is:2 Count of negatives is:2
Sum of positives is:931 Sum of negatives is:-1025
Please input a new value: 1
Location 2:
New value read in is: 1
Highest value is:917 Lowest value is:-789
Count of positives is:3 Count of negatives is:2
Sum of positives is:932 Sum of negatives is:-1025
Please input a new value:-67
Location 2:
New value read in is:-67
Highest value is:917 Lowest value is:-789
Count of positives is:3 Count of negatives is:3
Sum of positives is:932 Sum of negatives is:-1092
Please input a new value: 1001
Location 3:
New value read in is: 1001
Highest value is:917 Lowest value is:-789
Count of positives is:3 Count of negatives is:3
Sum of positives is:932 Sum of negatives is:-1092
Final output of the program.
Highest value is:917 Lowest value is:-789
Sum of positives is:932 Sum of negatives is:-1092
Mean of positives is:310.667 Mean of negatives is:-364
```

Figure 3.3 (Continued)

to see if the input statement is working correctly. Note that all the other values in the first trace output are the initial values of the variables set by the variable declarations in the program.

The second trace output is for Location 2. A trace is placed after the two sets of `if....else` statements and the accompanying computations, but before the end of the `while` loop and before the next input value. This allows you to see what changes were made to the variables for the minimum value, the maximum value, the sum of the positive values, and the sum of the negative values for each pass through the loop. Because the loop ends with a new input value, each pass through the loop is done with a different input value.

The third and final trace output statement is for Location 3. This final trace is placed after the `while` loop, after the last legal input is made and after the mean values are computed, so all the final values of variables can be checked. Those values should be the same values as in the normal program output at the end of the program.

Note that every one of these traces displays every variable in the program. This is acceptable for small programs, but it could be very cumbersome for large programs, because you have to insert very long trace statements all throughout the program, which means you get a lot of output displayed during the debugging process. In large programs, we recommend that you display, for a given trace statement, only the *critical variables*. Typically the critical variables are those variables that are being modified by the program at that particular point in the program. You don't need to keep displaying the other variables that are not being modified right now.

In summary, the design of a trace involves two decisions: what critical variables to display, and where to put the trace statements in the program. The critical variables can be chosen to be all the variables that are modified within a function or all the variables that are modified in a large block of code within a function, including the main function. What is "a large block of code"? Our rule of thumb is that no block of code should exceed the screen size of your computer, say 40-50 lines. This allows you to keep track of everything relevant to your trace on the screen at the same time.

In making the decision as to where a trace should be placed, it should be kept in mind that there are logical breaks in a program that should be checked—say, after an `if...else` statement combination or a short sequence of `if...else` statements. If your program has a long series of computational statements without control statements, put at least one trace on each computer screen's worth of code, and preferably a trace for every 10-15 lines of sequential code. It is also good to have a trace just before, during, and just after a `while` or `for` loop; and it is important to display the loop variable as well since it gets modified (or should be modified) each pass through the loop.

Finally, note that you don't have to actually print trace output in hard copy unless it is absolutely necessary. Just use the on-line display capability whenever possible (and save the forests!).

3.3   COMMON ERRORS DETECTABLE WITH BASIC TRACING

We now take a look at some fairly common errors that programmers make and see how they can be detected with tracing, and then corrected. We will

take the simple program shown in Fig. 3.2 and make some minor changes to it
that will cause errors.

Error 1 Failure to properly initialize variables

Let us look at Lines 8 and 9 in Fig. 3.2 and assume the variables highest_value
and `lowest_value` have been defined without initialization:

```
Line 8 (incorrect):        int highest_value;
Line 9 (incorrect):        int lowest_value;
Line 8 (correct):          int highest_value = MIN_VALUE-1;
Line 9 (correct):          int lowest_value = MAX_VALUE+1;
```

When we compile and run this program, we get incorrect results. The output
from this run is shown in Fig. 3.4. Let's take a look at the first trace output (Location 1) after the first value is input from the keyboard. The highest value is
displayed as 117293812 and the lowest value is 0 (shown in boldface in Fig.
3.4). These values represent the old values stored in the memory locations for
highest_value and lowest_value, respectively, and have no relevance to our
current program. In the original program, highest_value was initialized to
MIN_VALUE − 1 (-1001), which would be less than any legal value entered as
input, and thus would be replaced with the new value immediately. Similarly,
in the original program the lowest_value was initialized to MAX_VALUE + 1
(1001) and would be replaced with the first legal input value.

```
Program output:
Please input a new value: 917
Location 1:
New value read in is: 917
Highest value is:117293812 Lowest value is:0
Count of positives is:0 Count of negatives is:0
Sum of positives is:0 Sum of negatives is:0
Location 2:
New value read in is: 917
Highest value is: 117293812 Lowest value is:0
Count of positives is:1 Count of negatives is:0
Sum of positives is:917 Sum of negatives is:0
Please input a new value:-236
Location 2:
New value read in is:-236
Highest value is: 117293812 Lowest value is:-236
Count of positives is:1 Count of negatives is:1
Sum of positives is:917 Sum of negatives is:-236
Please input a new value: 14
```

Figure 3.4

Incorrect (partial) output with trace (Error 1)

```
Location 2:
New value read in is: 14
```
Highest value is: 117293812 Lowest value is:-236
```
Count of positives is:2 Count of negatives is:1
Sum of positives is:931 Sum of negatives is:-236
Please input a new value:.............
```

Figure 3.4 (Continued)

Unfortunately, the carryover value 117293812 in this version of the program is larger than any legal input value, and it remains the highest value throughout the entire execution. This is clearly shown in the trace output—the value 117293812 is illegal, but it is never changed by the program.

In the case of the lowest_value initialized at 0, the first negative number input (−236) replaces it, and this part of the program runs correctly after that point. However, if the inputs included only positive numbers, the value 0 would have remained unchanged during the execution and would have been incorrect. The trace may or may not cause you to catch this problem, but it would be helpful for you to see the initial value of 0 displayed and realize that it was not a good initial value. The error is corrected by initializing highest_value and lowest_value properly, as in Fig. 3.2, lines 8–9.

This example shows that the set of input data could have a direct bearing on whether or not a particular error will show up and be detected. The trace data helps to increase the probability that the error will be detected, but does not always guarantee it.

Error 2 Program logic error: switching comparison operators

This problem involves a logic error in the program shown in Fig. 3.2. In lines 22 and 25, let's assume the comparison operators < and > are reversed by accident.

```
Line 22 (incorrect):          if (new_value < highest_value)
Line 25 (incorrect):          if (new_value > lowest_value)
Line 22 (correct):            if (new_value > highest_value)
Line 25 (correct):            if (new_value < lowest_value)
```

The trace output in Fig. 3.5 shows that the highest value and lowest value do not change as new input values are read in. This tells the programmer that there might be an error in the logic of the if statements, which is indeed the case in this program. A quick check of the if statements should lead to making the proper corrections.

```
Program output:
Please input a new value: 917
Location 1:
New value read in is: 917
Highest value is:-1001 Lowest value is:1001
Count of positives is:0 Count of negatives is:0
Sum of positives is:0 Sum of negatives is:0
Location 2:
New value read in is: 917
Highest value is:-1001 Lowest value is:1001
Count of positives is:1 Count of negatives is:0
Sum of positives is:917 Sum of negatives is:0
Please input a new value:-236
Location 2:
New value read in is:-236
Highest value is:-1001 Lowest value is:1001
Count of positives is:1 Count of negatives is:1
Sum of positives is:917 Sum of negatives is:-236
Please input a new value: 14
Location 2:
New value read in is: 14
Highest value is:-1001 Lowest value is:1001
Count of positives is:2 Count of negatives is:1
Sum of positives is:931 Sum of negatives is:-236
Please input a new value:.........
```

Figure 3.5

Incorrect (partial) output with trace (Error 2)

Error 3 Program logic: off by one error

This problem is an example of the "off-by-one" error mentioned earlier in
Chapter 2. In line 28 let's assume the code if (new_value >= 0) is replaced by
the erroneous code if (new_value > 0) and the erroneous output is shown in
Fig. 3.6. This error, in which the count of positives is not properly incremented
(shown in boldface in Fig. 3.6), only occurs when the input value is zero.

```
Line 28 (incorrect):       if ( new_value > 0 )
Line 28 (correct):         if ( new_value >= 0 )
```

At this point in the execution of the program, note that the count of positives
has not been changed, but the count of negatives has been erroneously incremented. The trace shows that the program logic was incorrect for an input
value of 0. Data sets that do not include the value 0 will not show this error,
and thus it could elude detection for a long time.

```
Program output:
Please input a new value: 917
Location 1:
New value read in is: 917
Highest value is:-1001 Lowest value is:1001
Count of positives is:0 Count of negatives is:0
Sum of positives is:0 Sum of negatives is:0
Location 2:
New value read in is: 917
Highest value is:917 Lowest value is:917
Count of positives is:1 Count of negatives is:0
Sum of positives is:917 Sum of negatives is:0
Please input a new value:-236
Location 2:
New value read in is:-236
Highest value is:917 Lowest value is:-236
Count of positives is:1 Count of negatives is:1
Sum of positives is:917 Sum of negatives is:-236
Please input a new value: 14
Location 2:
New value read in is: 14
Highest value is:917 Lowest value is:-236
Count of positives is:2 Count of negatives is:1
Sum of positives is:931 Sum of negatives is:-236
Please input a new value:-789
Location 2:
New value read in is:-789
Highest value is:917 Lowest value is:-789
Count of positives is:2 Count of negatives is:2
Sum of positives is:931 Sum of negatives is:-1025
Please input a new value: 0
Location 2:
New value read in is: 0
Highest value is:917 Lowest value is:-789
Count of positives is:2 Count of negatives is:3
Sum of positives is:931 Sum of negatives is:-1025
Please input a new value:..........
```

Figure 3.6

Incorrect (partial) output with trace (Error 3)

Error 4 Division using integers

Lines 44 and 45 in the original program (Fig. 3.2) specify floating point division by casting each variable as a floating point number. Let's assume these two lines have been erroneously programmed to be a division between two integers:

```
Line 44 (incorrect):          mean_pos_values =
                              sum_pos_values/count_pos_values;
Line 45 (incorrect):          mean_neg_values =
                              sum_neg_values/count_neg_values;
Line 44 (correct):            mean_pos_values = float(sum_pos_values)
                              /float(count_pos_values);
Line 45 (correct):            mean_neg_values = float(sum_neg_values)
                              /float(count_neg_values);
```

The output of this modified program is shown in Fig. 3.7. It shows that the computation moves ahead correctly until the very last trace statement (Location 3, where the new value is given as 1001 to terminate the program). At this point the mean of positives is shown as the integer value 310. If we do a hand check of the sum of positive values (932) divided by the count of positive values (3), we get 310.67, which is the correct result. Thus tracing makes it easy to check the correctness of the arithmetic.

```
Program output:
Please input a new value: 917
Location 1:
New value read in is: 917
Highest value is:[[-]]1001 Lowest value is:1001
Count of positives is:0 Count of negatives is:0
Sum of positives is:0 Sum of negatives is:0
Location 2:
New value read in is: 917
Highest value is:917 Lowest value is:917
Count of positives is:1 Count of negatives is:0
Sum of positives is:917 Sum of negatives is:0
Please input a new value:-236
..........
Please input a new value: 14
..........
Please input a new value:-789
..........
Please input a new value: 1
..........
Please input a new value:-67
Location 2:
New value read in is:-67
Highest value is:917 Lowest value is:-789
Count of positives is:3 Count of negatives is:3
Sum of positives is:932 Sum of negatives is:-1092
```

Figure 3.7

Incorrect (partial) output with trace (Error 4)

```
Mean of positives is:0 Mean of negatives is:0
Please input a new value: 1001
Location 3:
New value read in is: 1001
Highest value is:917 Lowest value is:-789
Count of positives is:3 Count of negatives is:3
Sum of positives is:932 Sum of negatives is:-1092
Mean of positives is:310 Mean of negatives is:-364
Final output of the program.
Highest value is:917 Lowest value is:-789
Sum of positives is:931 Sum of negatives is:-1092
Mean of positives is:310 Mean of negatives is:-364
```

Figure 3.7 (Continued)

Error 5 Program logic error: poor use of `else`

Line 25 in the original program (Fig. 3.2) checks each new value against the current highest value and if the new value is larger, it replaces the old highest value with the new one. Then it checks to see if the same new value is smaller than the current lowest value, and it replaces the old lowest value with the new one. We modify the second `if` (line 25) to be `else if`, which checks for the new value lower than the current lowest value only if the first test on highest values (line 22) fails.

```
Line 25 (incorrect):        else if (new_value < lowest_value)
Line 25 (correct):          if (new_value < lowest_value)
```

The output for this modified program is shown in Fig. 3.8. The trace output for Location 1 indicates that the results are correct so far. However, the first trace output for Location 2 shows that while the highest value has correctly been changed from −1001 (initialized value) to 917 (the first input value), the lowest value remains unchanged at 1001 (the initialized value). It should also have the value 917 at this time, but does not, which is an error. The second trace output for Location 2 corrects this error, luckily, and shows −236 as the current lowest value.

While we were lucky in this case, if the first value input had been a very low negative value—for instance −999—it would have replaced the old highest value because it is larger than −1001. However, it would not have been checked for lowest value during this iteration of the for loop and would be lost forever. This problem would be easily found by comparing the trace at Location 1 with the first trace at Location 2.

```
Program output:
Please input a new value: 917
Location 1:
New value read in is: 917
Highest value is:-1001 Lowest value is:1001
Count of positives is:0 Count of negatives is:0
Sum of positives is:0 Sum of negatives is:0
Location 2:
New value read in is: 917
Highest value is:917 Lowest value is:1001
Count of positives is:1 Count of negatives is:0
Sum of positives is:917 Sum of negatives is:0
Please input a new value:-236
Location 2:
New value read in is:-236
Highest value is:917 Lowest value is:-236
Count of positives is:1 Count of negatives is:1
Sum of positives is:917 Sum of negatives is:-236
Please input a new value:..........
```

Figure 3.8

Incorrect (partial) output using trace (Error 5)

3.4 TRACE ON AND OFF FLAG

The basic tracing method shown in Sec. 3.1 can be made more efficient. It is cumbersome to turn off the tracing when you just want to run the program by itself. You either have to go through the program and delete all the trace statements, or you have to add comments around all trace statements to "comment them out" so they won't be executed. The commenting approach is more useful since it allows you to quickly put the tracing back in without having to type the trace statements all in again, but the use of a bool variable, or flag, to turn tracing on and off is even better.

Fig. 3.9 shows a code segment of how a bool tracing flag, called trace_on, can be implemented. The declaration for trace_on is made before main since it is a global variable. Note that this is a valid exception to the "never use global variables" rule, because in this case the global variable trace_on is only used for debugging purposes, and it can be deleted from the program once it runs correctly. The variable trace_on is initialized to "true" (after line 2) to allow debug tracing to be executed in the program. If you want to turn off all debugging, simply reinitialize trace_on to "false". The tracing statements in the example program are the same as before, but the revised program has an extra if statement inserted in each location (after lines 19, 39, and 43 in Fig. 3.2) to check to see whether debug tracing is turned on or off. See Fig. 3.10 for all the trace_on code inserts.

```
1 #include <iostream>
2 using namespace std;
2.1 //debugging variable trace_on
2.2 bool trace_on = true;
2.3
3 int main()
4 {
5     const int MIN_VALUE = -1000;
6     const int MAX_VALUE = 1000;
7     int new_value;
8     int highest_value = MIN_VALUE-1;
9     int lowest_value = MAX_VALUE+1;
10    int count_pos_values = 0;
11    int count_neg_values = 0;
12    int sum_pos_values = 0;
13    int sum_neg_values = 0;
14
15    float mean_pos_values = 0.;
16    float mean_neg_values = 0.;
17
18    cout << "Please input a new value: ";
19    cin >> new_value;
19.01  //insert test to see if trace_on is true before tracing
19.02  if (trace_on)
19.03      //debug trace statement
19.04      cout << endl << "Location 1:" << endl
19.05          << "New value read in is: " << new_value << endl
19.06          << "Highest value is:" << highest_value
19.07          << " Lowest value is:" << lowest_value << endl
19.08          << "Count of positives is:" << count_pos_values
19.09          << " Count of negatives is:" << count_neg_values
                  << endl
19.10          << "Sum of positives is:" << sum_pos_values
19.11          << " Sum of negatives is:" << sum_neg_values << endl
                  << endl;
```

......

Figure 3.9

First few lines of example program in Fig. 3.2 with trace flag trace_on code.

```
/*Debugging Example - This is the same example program as Figs. 3.1
and 3.2, but with flags and function calls for tracing */
1 #include <iostream>
2 using namespace std;
2.1 //debugging variables and function prototype
2.2 bool trace_on = true;
2.3 int trace_loc = 0;
2.4 void trace_display (int,int,int,int,int,int,int,int);
2.5
3 int main()
4 {
5     const int MIN_VALUE = -1000;
6     const int MAX_VALUE = 1000;
7     int new_value;
8     int highest_value = MIN_VALUE-1;
9     int lowest_value = MAX_VALUE+1;
10    int count_pos_values = 0;
11    int count_neg_values = 0;
12    int sum_pos_values = 0;
13    int sum_neg_values = 0;
14    float mean_pos_values = 0.;
15    float mean_neg_values = 0.;
16
17    cout << "Please input a new value: ";
18    cin >> new_value;
19
19.1   //debug trace statement
19.2   if (trace_on)
19.3        trace_display (1, new_value, highest_value, lowest_value,
19.4                    count_pos_values, count_neg_values, sum_pos_values,
19.5                    sum_neg_values);
19.6
20    while (new_value >= MIN_VALUE && new_value <= MAX_VALUE)
21    {
22            if (new_value > highest_value)
23                    highest_value = new_value;
24
25            if (new_value < lowest_value)
26                    lowest_value = new_value;
```

Figure 3.10

Example program with the debug on/off flag and function trace calls

```
27
28                  if (new_value >= 0)
29                  {
30                          count_pos_values++;
31                          sum_pos_values += new_value;
32                  }
33
34                  else
35                  {
36                          count_neg_values++;
37                          sum_neg_values += new_value;
38                  }
39
39.1       //debug trace statement
39.2       if (trace_on)
39.3           trace_display (2, new_value, highest_value, lowest_value,
39.4               count_pos_values, count_neg_values, sum_pos_values,
39.5               sum_neg_values);
39.6
40                  cout << "Please input a new value: ";
41                  cin >> new_value;
42
43      }
43.1    //debug trace statement
43.2    if (trace_on)
43.3        trace_display (3, new_value, highest_value, lowest_value
43.4            count_pos_values, count_neg_values, sum_pos_values,
43.5            sum_neg_values);
43.6
44      mean_pos_values = float(sum_pos_values)/float(count_pos_values);
45      mean_neg_values = float(sum_neg_values)/float(count_neg_values);
46
47      //program output statement
48      cout << endl << "Final output of the program." << endl
49                      << "Highest value is:" << highest_value
50                      << " Lowest value is:" << lowest_value << endl
51                      << "Sum of positives is:" << sum_pos_values
52                      << " Sum of negatives is:" << sum_neg_values << endl
53                      << "Mean of positives is:" << mean_pos_values
54                      << " Mean of negatives is:"
                        << mean_neg_values << endl << endl;
55
```

Figure 3.10 (Continued)

```
56        return 0;
57 }
58
57.01   void trace_display (int trace_loc, int new_value,
57.02       int highest_value, int lowest_value,
57.03       int count_pos_values, int count_neg_values,
57.04       int sum_neg_values, int sum_neg_values)
57.05     {
57.06   cout << endl << "Location " << trace_loc << ":" << endl
57.07         << "New value read in is: " << new_value << endl
57.08         << "Highest value is:" << highest_value
57.09         << " Lowest value is:" << lowest_value << endl
57.10         << "Count of positives is:" << count_pos_values
57.11         << " Count of negatives is:" << count_neg_values
              << endl
57.12         << "Sum of positives is:" << sum_pos_values
57.13         << " Sum of negatives is:" << sum_neg_values
              << endl << endl;
57.14
57.15   return;
57.16 }
```

Figure 3.10 (Continued)

3.5 TRACING USING FUNCTION CALLS

It would be nice to be able to have the tracing statements just call a function that listed the variables to be displayed, instead of having to type in the long tracing statements many times in the program.

You could make each trace statement a call to your debugging function, which will then display the critical variables you want to track. Line 2.4 of our modified program in Fig. 3.10 shows the function prototype for such a debugging function, which we will call `trace_display`. The function body is shown in lines 57.01 to 57.16, and the function calls to `trace_display` from the main function are shown starting at lines 19.3, 39.3, and 43.3.

Let's look at the `trace_display` function body first. Lines 57.01 to 57.04 show the function heading. It is a void function with no value returned except the variables being displayed. The first variable in the list is `trace_loc`, the location number, which must be specified as either 1, 2, or 3 in our example from the function calls for the three locations of trace statements in main, lines 19.3, 39.3, and 43.3 (Fig. 3.10). All the remaining variables in the function heading are the same as the variables we displayed in the basic tracing method in Fig. 3.2.

The real advantages of making function calls for tracing are simplicity and flexibility. It *simplifies* the insertion of trace statements in the program because you just have to insert the `if` statements for the flags, and then just do the function call. It is *flexible* because you can define different functions for different sets of critical variables and just make minor adjustments in the calls to those functions.

We highly recommend the use of the `cout` statements, tracing on/off flags, and trace function calls as your most important tools for debugging with tracing.

3.6   TRACING FOR DATA IN ARRAYS

Debugging for programs with arrays is almost the same as for those programs without arrays, but you must think about the special problem of an array index being out of bounds. If you have an array of 10 components declared as

```
float x[10] = {1.0, 2.0, 2.5, 3.7, 4.2, -3.6, -.4, 8.4, 12.3, -.9};
```

then you must remember that the 10 components are x[0], x[1], x[2],........,x[9]. If you try to store a value into x[10], for instance, you would be storing that value into another memory location that may have been allocated to another variable in your program, which would cause an error. Furthermore, any use of the variable x[10] would also be in error. We can use tracing to detect these types of errors quickly.

Fig. 3.11 shows a new program that accomplishes the same task as the previous program we showed in Figs. 3.1 to 3.10, except that the six input values we read in for the first program (using the `cin` statement) are now presented explicitly in the new program to initialize an array a[ARRAY_SIZE] in line 15. The debug tracing statements in the new program are similar to the ones in Fig. 3.10 that include flags and function calls. The difference between the new function calls and the previous program's function calls are that the new function calls include the array component name a[i], and the array subscript i instead of new_value (see lines 18.3, 41.3, and 50.3 in Fig. 3.11). The function heading for trace_display is shown on lines 66.01 through 66.04.

```
/*Debugging Example - This is the same example as in Fig. 3.1, except
we are now using arrays to hold the initial values to be manipulated
instead of using cin to input them. This version also includes func-
tion calls for tracing and the debug on/off flag*/
1 #include <iostream>
2 using namespace std;
2.1    //debugging variables and function prototype
2.2    bool trace_on = true;
2.3    int trace_loc = 0;
2.4    void trace_display (int,int,int,int,int,int,int,int,int);
2.5
3  int main()
```

Figure 3.11

Example program using arrays and debug tracing functions

```
4   {
5       const int ARRAY_SIZE = 6;
6       const int MIN_VALUE = -1000;
7       const int MAX_VALUE = 1000;
8       int a[ARRAY_SIZE] = {917, -236, 14, -789, 0, -67};
9       int highest_value = MIN_VALUE-1;
10      int lowest_value = MAX_VALUE+1;
11      int count_pos_values = 0;
12      int count_neg_values = 0;
13      int sum_pos_values = 0;
14      int sum_neg_values = 0;
15      int i = 0;
16      float mean_pos_values = 0.;
17      float mean_neg_values = 0.;
18
18.1 //debug trace statement
18.2 if (trace_on)
18.3        trace_display (1, i, a[i], highest_value,
18.4            lowest_value, count_pos_values,
18.5            count_neg_values, sum_pos_values, sum_neg_values);
18.6
19      for (i = 0; i < ARRAY_SIZE; i++)
20      {
21
22              if (a[i] >= MIN_VALUE && a[i] <= MAX_VALUE)
23              {
24                      if (a[i] > highest_value)
25                              highest_value = a[i];
26
27                      if (a[i] < lowest_value)
28                              lowest_value = a[i];
29
30                      if (a[i] >= 0)
31                      {
32                              count_pos_values++;
33                              sum_pos_values += a[i];
34                      }
35
36                      else
37                      {
38                              count_neg_values++;
39                              sum_neg_values += a[i];
40                      }
41
```

Figure 3.11 (Continued)

```
41.1                        //debug trace statement
41.2                        if (trace_on)
41.3                            trace_display (2, i, a[i],
41.4                                highest_value, lowest_value,
41.5                                count_pos_values, count_neg_values,
41.6                                sum_pos_values,
41.7                                sum_neg_values);
42              }
43
44          else
45          {
46                      //fails error check - not within bounds
47                      cout << "ERROR: a[i] value is out of bounds: "
                            << a[i] << endl;
48                      exit(1);
49          }
50    }
50.1 //debug trace statement
50.2 if (trace_on)
50.3     trace_display (3, i, a[i], highest_value, lowest_value,
50.4         count_pos_values, count_neg_values, sum_pos_values,
50.5         sum_neg_values);
50.6
51
52   mean_pos_values = float(sum_pos_values)/float(count_pos_values);
53   mean_neg_values = float(sum_neg_values)/float(count_neg_values);
54
55   //program output statement
56   cout << endl << "Final output of the program." << endl
57                   << "Highest value is:" << highest_value
58                   << " Lowest value is:" << lowest_value << endl
59                   << "Sum of positives is:" << sum_pos_values
60                   << " Sum of negatives is:" << sum_neg_values << endl
61                   << "Mean of positives is:" << mean_pos_values
62                   << " Mean of negatives is:" << mean_neg_values
                     << endl << endl;
63
64   return 0;
65   }
66
66.01 void trace_display (int trace_loc, int i, int a_value,
66.02     int highest_value, int lowest_value,
66.03     int count_pos_values,int count_neg_values,
66.04     int sum_pos_values,int sum_neg_values)
```

Figure 3.11 (Continued)

```
66.05
66.06 {
66.07         cout << endl << "Location " << trace_loc << ":"<< endl
66.08              << "New array component value: " << a_value
                   << " and index value: " << i << endl
66.09              << "Highest value is:" << highest_value
66.10              << " Lowest value is:" << lowest_value << endl
66.11              << "Count of positives is:" << count_pos_values
66.12              << " Count of negatives is:" << count_neg_values
                   << endl
66.13              << "Sum of positives is:" << sum_pos_values
66.14              << " Sum of negatives is:" << sum_neg_values
                   << endl << endl;
66.15
66.16         return;
66.17 }
```

Figure 3.11 (Continued)

The trace output for the new program is shown in Fig. 3.12, and the output is correct. However, the output for Location 3 (near the bottom), which occurs after the for loop is exited and just after the mean values are computed, shows an odd value as the "new array component value." Notice that the array is defined as a[ARRAY_SIZE] with ARRAY_SIZE defined as 6, so that a[6] would be out of bounds. We exit the for loop when the index value reaches 6, and that is the value used for the Location 3 trace. However, the program no longer uses this array at this point, so this arbitrary value of 1127219200 for a[6] is never accessed or used.

```
Program output:
Location 1:
New array element value: 917 and index value: 0
Highest value is:-1001 Lowest value is:1001
Count of positives is:0 Count of negatives is:0
Sum of positives is:0 Sum of negatives is:0
Location 2:
New array element value: 917 and index value: 0
Highest value is:917 Lowest value is:917
Count of positives is:1 Count of negatives is:0
Sum of positives is:917 Sum of negatives is:0
```

Figure 3.12

Correct output for example program using arrays

```
Location 2:
New array element value: -236 and index value: 1
Highest value is:917 Lowest value is:-236
Count of positives is:1 Count of negatives is:1
Sum of positives is:917 Sum of negatives is: -236
Location 2:
New array element value: 14 and index value: 2
Highest value is:917 Lowest value is: -236
Count of positives is:2 Count of negatives is:1
Sum of positives is:931 Sum of negatives is: -236
Location 2:
New array element value: [[-]]789 and index value: 3
Highest value is:917 Lowest value is: -789
Count of positives is:2 Count of negatives is:2
Sum of positives is:931 Sum of negatives is: -1025
Location 2:
New array element value: 1 and index value: 4
Highest value is:917 Lowest value is: -789
Count of positives is:3 Count of negatives is:2
Sum of positives is:932 Sum of negatives is: -1025
Location 2:
New array element value: -67 and index value: 5
Highest value is:917 Lowest value is: -789
Count of positives is:3 Count of negatives is:3
Sum of positives is:932 Sum of negatives is: -1092
Location 3:
New array element value: 1127219200 and index value: 6
Highest value is:917 Lowest value is: -789
Count of positives is:3 Count of negatives is:3
Sum of positives is:932 Sum of negatives is: -1092
Final output of the program.
Highest value is:917 Lowest value is: -789
Sum of positives is:932 Sum of negatives is: -1092
Mean of positives is:310.667 Mean of negatives is: -364
```

Figure 3.12 (Continued)

Error 6 Array index out of bounds

Let's look at a situation in which the index value of 6 is used in the program, and an error is produced that we need to detect. Let's assume the program is erroneously modified as follows:

```
Line 19 (incorrect):        for (i = 0; i <= ARRAY_SIZE; i++)
Line 19 (correct):          for (i = 0; i < ARRAY_SIZE; i++)
```

We have changed "<" to "<=" in line 19 so that component a[6] is now used in the program when it shouldn't be. This is another example of an "off-by-one" error. The trace output for this program modification and execution is shown in Fig. 3.13. This error does not cause a system crash because the value for a[6] happens to be 1, a legal value in the program. However, the error is detectable in the trace output for Location 2. If you forget that an index of 6 is illegal for this array, you might detect the problem two lines later when the count of positives is 4 and the count of negatives is 3, adding up to 7. Since the array size is only 6, this would tell you that there has been an error. If the value for a[6] had been very large or very small, and out of range of legal values, the program would have stopped and generated correct results (even with the bad code!). In this case, the bad code just wasn't executed this time, so no error occurred. This kind of problem is a good reminder of the need to thoroughly test our programs before putting them into production.

```
Program output:
Location 1:
New array element value: 917 & index value: 0
Highest value is:-1001 Lowest value is:1001
Count of positives is:0 Count of negatives is:0
Sum of positives is:0 Sum of negatives is:0
Location 2:
New array element value: 917 and index value: 0
Highest value is:917 Lowest value is:917
Count of positives is:1 Count of negatives is:0
Sum of positives is:917 Sum of negatives is:0
Location 2:
New array element value: -236 and index value: 1
Highest value is:917 Lowest value is: -236
Count of positives is:1 Count of negatives is:1
Sum of positives is:917 Sum of negatives is: -236
Location 2:
New array element value: 14 and index value: 2
Highest value is:917 Lowest value is: -236
Count of positives is:2 Count of negatives is:1
Sum of positives is:931 Sum of negatives is: -236
Location 2:
New array element value: -789 and index value: 3
Highest value is:917 Lowest value is: -789
Count of positives is:2 Count of negatives is:2
Sum of positives is:931 Sum of negatives is: -1025
```

Figure 3.13

Incorrect output for array version of program with trace (Error 6)

```
Location 2:
New array element value: 1 and index value: 4
Highest value is:917 Lowest value is:-789
Count of positives is:3 Count of negatives is:2
Sum of positives is:932 Sum of negatives is:-1025
Location 2:
New array element value: -67 and index value: 5
Highest value is:917 Lowest value is:-789
Count of positives is:3 Count of negatives is:3
Sum of positives is:932 Sum of negatives is:-1092
Location 2:
New array element value: 1 and index value: 6
Highest value is:917 Lowest value is:-789
Count of positives is:4 Count of negatives is:3
Sum of positives is:933 Sum of negatives is:-1092
Location 3:
New array element value: -2147483645 and index value: 7
Highest value is:917 Lowest value is:-789
Count of positives is:4 Count of negatives is:3
Sum of positives is:933 Sum of negatives is:-1092
Final output of the program.
Highest value is:917 Lowest value is:-789
Sum of positives is:933 Sum of negatives is:-1092
Mean of positives is:233.25 Mean of negatives is:-364
```

Figure 3.13 (Continued)

Error 7 Bad use of `while` instead of `if`

The array program in Fig. 3.11 would be wrong if the programmer had used a `while` loop in line 22 instead of an `if` statement, which would eliminate the "else" lines 44–49 for the error check:

```
Incorrect line 22:     while (a[i] >= MIN_VALUE && a[i] <= MAX_VALUE)
Correct line 22:       if (a[i] >= MIN_VALUE && a[i] <= MAX_VALUE)
```

If the incorrect form of line 22 were used, the program would go into an infinite loop within the `while` block. The output of this execution is shown in Fig. 3.14. The output has some clues that the program has gone into an infinite loop. The first clue is that the index value (i) for the `for` loop (line 19) never changes from 0 for each trace output. This means that the end of the `for` loop is never reached and therefore the loop index (i) is never incremented. The second clue is that the new value that is read (917 in this case) never changes, which tells you that the you never advance in the array beyond a[0].

```
Program output:
Location 1:
```
New array element value:917 and index value:0
```
Highest value is:-1001 Lowest value is:1001
Count of positives is:0 Count of negatives is:0
Sum of positives is:0 Sum of negatives is:0
Location 2:
```
New array element value:917 and index value:0
```
Highest value is:917 Lowest value is:917
Count of positives is:1 Count of negatives is:0
Sum of positives is:917 Sum of negatives is:0
Location 2:
```
New array element value:917 and index value:0
```
Highest value is:917 Lowest value is:917
Count of positives is:2 Count of negatives is:0
Sum of positives is:1834 Sum of negatives is:0
Location 2:
```
New array element value:917 and index value:0
```
Highest value is:917 Lowest value is:917
Count of positives is:3 Count of negatives is:0
Sum of positives is:2751 Sum of negatives is:0
Location 2:………….etc.
```

Figure 3.14

Incorrect (partial) output for array version with trace (Error 7)

Detecting the error (finding the infinite loop) does not always indicate what it is that caused the problem, so further investigation would be needed to find the cause. The infinite loop for the `while` statement should make you question why that loop is there in addition to the `for` loop, and reexamine what is happening in the program. Eventually you would realize that a double loop is unnecessary and the inner loop should be eliminated.

3.7   WHERE TO INSERT THE TRACES AND WHAT VARIABLES TO DISPLAY

In this section we summarize with some rules of thumb about where to insert the traces into the program code and what variables to display for each type of trace. Think of this as a checklist that can be added to or subtracted from, depending on the specific conditions in your program code.

1 Sequential code (no control statements)
  *display critical variables at the end of each 10–15 lines of purely sequential code.

2 If-else statements
  *display critical variables just before and after `if` and `else` conditions

3 `while` and `for` loops
  *display critical variables just before and after `while` or `for` blocks
  *display critical variables within `while` or `for` loops consistently just before or after the increment or decrement of the loop counter.
  *display the loop counter

4 Functions
  *display all parameters before and after each function entry
  *display all parameters before and after each function exit

5 Arrays
  *display array components and array index values

6 Character strings
  *display critical variables before and after each use of a string function.

7 Structs and class objects
  *display critical variables in a struct or class object just after initialization and any update, including updates from constructors

8 Pointers
  *display pointer values before and after each update of a pointer. Pointer addresses may not be meaningful at first, but keep track of them for comparative purposes to make sure the values are not corrupted during the program execution.

3.8   USING THE `ASSERT` MACRO

In this section, we will look at the standard C++ `assert` feature, another handy debugging tool. Discussion of its use is included in this chapter because it provides a way to stop execution of a program mid-stream during the debugging process. Note that if a program run is stopped using `assert`, the run cannot be resumed without totally restarting the program. `Assert` also does not allow you to examine variables. It does allow you to very easily and quickly stop a run when a specific error occurs. In programming, the idea of an assertion means that the programmer asserts that some condition must be true. The basic concept here is that execution is stopped if some condition is not true.

`Assert` is defined as a macro (which usually are not covered until more advanced C++ coursework), but we call it much as we do when using other C++ functions. First, we must include the appropriate header file, `cassert`. Then, the call looks like the following:

```
assert (<expression>);
```

If the expression is *true* (has a nonzero value), the call to `assert` executes, and then the flow of control moves on to the next statement in the program. If the expression is *false* (has a zero value), after `assert` executes, the program halts immediately, and an error message is printed to indicate that the assertion has *failed*.

Let's look at a brief example. The following program is intended to open a text file, read one integer from that file, print it, and then close the file. Let's say that while debugging, you would like the program to simply halt if the file does not open properly. We can achieve this using the following code:

```
#include <iostream>
#include <fstream>
#include <cassert>
using namespace std;
int main ( )
{
    int number;
    ifstream inFile;
    inFile.open ("datafile.txt");
    assert (inFile);
    inFile >> number;
    cout << number;
    inFile.close ( );
    return 0;
}
```

If we run this program, and the file fails to open, the program run will stop and we will see an error message like the following:

```
Assertion (inFile) failed in "myprog.cpp" at line 11
```

Note that *assert* calls can be left in your program after you are finished debugging, but effectively they are turned *off* by inserting the following line in your program prior to the line that includes the cassert header file:

```
#define NDEBUG
```

This line, a "define directive" for the compiler, tells it to turn off all `assert` calls in the program so that they simply will not execute.

`Assert` is thus very convenient to use. You can write as many `assert` calls as you would like to in your program, then deactivate them all using this one line of code. Then, if you want to turn the `assert` calls back on later for more debugging, you can simply remove this line. This is very convenient for large programs undergoing frequent change, as programmers can turn this debugging tool on and off, as needed. Note that `assert` calls should always be deactivated before a program is provided to its actual end users.

CHAPTER 4

Trace Debugging for More Advanced C++ Constructs

4.1 CHAPTER OBJECTIVES

- To learn how to debug more advanced C++ constructs, such as strings, pointers, and structs
- To apply the debugging techniques to object-oriented programming using classes

4.2 STRINGS

String variables are declared in the same manner as other variables like `int`, `float`, `double`, and `bool`. However, strings serve many more purposes than do numeric data and use a number of built-in C++ functions for assignment, concatenation, finding the string length, finding a substring, and comparing strings, to name a few.

As we stated in Section 3.7, debugging traces can be inserted to display critical string variables before and after each use of a string function. This is illustrated in detail in Fig. 4.1, which shows the C++ source code to illustrate all the string functions mentioned previously. Trace statements are shown in boldface so we know the values of each string variable before and after its use in a string manipulation operation. A function called `testparam` is defined to illustrate the testing of string variables as both call-by-value and call-by-reference function parameters. Another function called `alpha_to_integer` (roughly equivalent to the C++ function `atoi`) is defined to illustrate the conversion of a string data

51

type—consisting of some number of positive digits—into an integer data type.

We display the initial values of five string variables, word1 through word5, using the cout statements in lines 24–28. The output of these values is shown in lines 2-6 of the output, shown after the code (fig. 4.1).

```
/*Debugging Example This program illustrates possible debugging code
insertions that would be useful for testing string manipulation
statements and string function calls. The program output is shown
following the program listing.*/
1   #include <iostream>
2   #include <string>
3   #include <cmath>
4   using namespace std;
5
6   //function prototypes
7   void testparam(string, string, string&);
8   int alpha_to_integer (string);
9
10  int main()
11  {
12      string word1 = "Hail";
13      string word2 = "my";
14      string word3 = "Chief!";
15      string word4;
16      string word5 = "456";
17      string nextsymbol1;
18      string nextsymbol2;
19      string nextsymbol3;
20      int result = 0;
21
22      cout << "BEGINNING OF TEST STRING PROGRAM OUTPUT." << endl;
23
24      cout << "word1 (string) is: " << word1 << endl;
25      cout << "word2 (string) is: " << word2 << endl;
26      cout << "word3 (string) is: " << word3 << endl;
27      cout << "word4 (string) is: " << word4 << endl;
28      cout << "word5 (string) is: " << word5 << endl << endl;
29
30      word4 = word1 + " to the " + word3;
31      cout << "word4 concatenates word1 & word3 with \" to the \" in
32      between: " << endl << word4 << endl;
33      if (word1 < word3)
34              cout << "word1 is less than word3." << endl;
35      else
```

Figure 4.1

Example program and output for testing string functions

```
36            cout << "word1 is not less than word3." << endl;
37    word4 = word3;
38    cout << "Value of word4 (set to word3) is now: " << word4
39            << endl << endl;
40
41    testparam(word1, word2, word3);
42  cout << "Return from function testparam: word1, word2, word3: "
43            << endl; << word1 << " " << word2 << " " << word3 << endl
44
45
46    nextsymbol1 = word1.substr(0,1);
47    nextsymbol2 = word1.substr(1,1);
48    nextsymbol3 = word1.substr(2,1);
49    cout << "Result of substring scan for first 3 "
50            << " symbols of word1 is: "
51            << nextsymbol1 << " " << nextsymbol2 << " "
52            << nextsymbol3 << endl;
53
54    cout << "word3 string length is: " << word3.length() << endl;
55    cout << "The substring of word3, index 3, length 2: "
56            << word3.substr(3,2) << endl;
57    word3 = word3 + word3;
58    cout << "The concatenation of word3 to itself is: "
59            << word3 << endl;
60    cout << "word3 string length is now: " << word3.length()
61            << endl << endl;
62
63    result = alpha_to_integer(word5);
64    cout << "Result of converting string word5 to an integer is: "
65            << result << endl << endl;
66    cout << "END OF TEST STRING PROGRAM OUTPUT." << endl;
67    return 0;
68 }
69
70 void testparam(string wordx, string wordy, string& wordz)
71 {
72    cout << "Entering the function testparam." << endl;
73
74    wordz = wordx + wordz;
75 }
76
77 int alpha_to_integer (string wordx)
78 {
79    int i;
80    int stringLength = wordx.length();
```

Figure 4.1 (Continued)

```
81      int number = 0;
82      char ch;
83
84      cout << "Entering the alpha_to_integer function." << endl;
85      for (i=0; i < stringLength; i++)
86      {
87              ch = wordx[i] - '0';
88              number = number + ch*pow(10.0, stringLength - i -1);
89              cout << "number is currently: " << number << endl;
90      }
91      return number;
92 }                        //end of example program code
```

```
1  BEGINNING OF TEST STRING PROGRAM OUTPUT.
2  word1 (string) is: Hail
3  word2 (string) is: my
4  word3 (string) is: Chief!
5  word4 (string) is:
6  word5 (string) is: 456
7
8  word4 concatenates word1 & word3 with " to the " in between:
9  between: Hail to the Chief!
10  word1 is not less than word3.
11 Value of word4 (set to word3) is now: Chief!
12
13 Entering the function testparam.
14 Return from function testparam: word1, word2, word3:
15 Hail my HailChief!
16
17 Result of substring scan for first 3 symbols of word1 is: H a i
18 word3 string length is: 10
19 The substring of word3, index 3, length 2 is: lC
20 The concatenation of word3 to itself is: HailChief!HailChief!
21 word3 string length is now: 20
22
23 Entering the alpha_to_integer function.
24 number is currently: 400
25 number is currently: 450
26 number is currently: 456
27 Result of converting string word5 to integer is: 456
28
29 END OF TEST STRING PROGRAM OUTPUT.
```

Figure 4.1 (Continued)

Concatenation is illustrated in line 30. The trace statement in lines 31–32 produces the output in line 8, which verifies that the word "and" is successfully inserted between word1 and word2.

String comparison is made in line 33, and the output is shown in line 10, verifying that the value of the first letter of word1, "A", is less than the value of the first letter of word3, "G." Simple string assignment is shown in line 37 in which word4 is set to the current value of word3, "Gamma." The output of this test is shown in line 11.

Strings as parameters to a function are tested in the function call of line 40 and the function "testparam" in lines 70–75. We see that word1 is renamed wordx in the function, and that word2 is renamed wordy. Word3 is renamed wordz in the function and is also defined as a call-by-reference parameter to allow it to be changed by the function. The function then defines wordz (word3 in main) as the concatenation of wordx (word1 in main) and wordz (word3 in main). When the function is entered during execution, that fact is displayed in line 13 using the code in line 72. After the function returns to main, the result of the function (the previous values for word1 and word2 and the new value for word3) is displayed in the output line 14 using the cout statement in lines 42–44 in main.

The substring and length functions are illustrated in lines 46–61 in Fig. 4.1, with the output shown in lines 17–21. When word3 is concatenated with itself, its length is doubled from 10 to 20.

The last segment of code in Fig. 4.1 is the function call (line 63) to alpha_to_integer which converts the string word5 (value "456") to the integer 456. Trace statements in the function are shown in lines 84 and 89. Line 23 of the test string program output shows the output for the function entry statement. The output for the evolution of values for the variable "number" is shown in output lines 24–26, and the return value for "number" is shown in output line 27.

Note that in line 82 the character variable ch must be specified as a char and not as a string—otherwise, line 88 would generate a syntax error because a string variable ch would not be convertible to double to complete the multiplication with the double function pow. Note that no casting of stringLength is required in line 88 because C++ automatically converts integers to double before executing pow.

4.3 POINTERS

A pointer is an address of some variable or constant in C++. If the content of the pointer is NULL, then the pointer points to nothing (i.e. it contains no address). You can assign pointers to other pointers and use pointers in arithmetic expressions. Remember also that array names are actually treated as pointers so that array names used as function parameters are actually pointers.

A pointer (called mypointer) to an integer variable (called myvariable) initialized to 100 is declared as follows:

```
int myvariable = 100;
int* mypointer = &myvariable;          //alternate form:
                                       //int *mypointer = &myvariable;
```

The asterisk symbol (*) is used to designate a pointer. The ampersand symbol (&) is called the *address operator*, and the expression &myvariable means "the address of myvariable." When the asterisk symbol is used next to a pointer in an expression, it is called the *dereferencing operator* and means "take the pointer value, an address, and find the value of the variable at that address". For instance, the expression

```
int x = 0;
x = *mypointer - 15;
cout << "The value of x is now: " << x << endl;
```

will display the value *85* for the variable *x*.

However, dropping the dereferencing operator from the second statement will result in a syntax error.

If we replace the second statement with

```
x = mypointer - 15;
```

we will get a syntax error cannot convert int* to int. Addresses should only be stored in declared pointers, and normal integer (or floating point, etc.) values should be stored in declared integer (or declared floating point, etc.) variables.

Programs with pointers can be debugged in a straightforward manner using the tracing techniques of Chapter 3 to record the values of pointers and other variables before and after they are read or updated by the program. In Fig. 4.2 a simple swap program is presented to illustrate the use of pointers. Tracing statements are shown in boldface type to help visualize how the pointer variables are changing. Lines 7 and 8 show the initial values of two variables, mydata and yourdata. In line 14 the main function calls the swap function with the addresses of mydata and yourdata as the calling parameters. The main code in the swap function is shown in lines 28–30. Here, the integer variable temp is set to the current value of the pointer variable by the mine pointer, which is the variable in main called mydata. Its current value is 999, and then the code on line 29 in the swap function

```
*mine = *yours;
```

is equivalent to the main function assignment

```
mydata = yourdata;
```

Finally, the code on line 30,

```
*yours = temp;
```

puts the temp value 999 into the variable pointed to yours—that is, yourdata.

```
/*Debugging Example This program swaps the values of two integers in
main. It uses pointers as parameters in the swap function to access
the original data in main. */
1 #include <iostream>
2 using namespace std;
3 void swap (int*, int* );     //swap function prototype
4
5 int main()
6 {
7      int mydata = 999;
8      int yourdata = 1221;
9      cout << "START OF MAIN (OUTPUT)." << endl;
10     cout << "mydata (address) = " << &mydata
11          << " yourdata (address) = " << &yourdata << endl;
12     cout << "mydata = " <<mydata << " yourdata = " << yourdata
13          << endl;                              //prints 999 & 1221
14     swap (&mydata, &yourdata);       //calls swap with int addresses
15     cout << "mydata = " <<mydata << " yourdata = " << yourdata
16          << endl;                              //prints 1221 & 999
17     cout << "END OF MAIN (OUTPUT)." << endl;
18     return 0;
19 }
20
21 void swap (int* mine, int* yours) //declares pointers to integers
22 {
23     int temp = 0;
24     cout << endl << "Entering swap function." << endl;
25     cout << "mine (value) = " << mine << " yours (value) = "
26          << yours << endl;
27     cout << "Before the swap: temp = " << temp
28          << " *mine (value) = " << *mine
29              << " *yours (value) = " << *yours << endl;
30     temp = *mine;      //mine points to "mydata" in main
31                        //(value of 999), stores 999 in temp
32     *mine = *yours;    //yours points to "yourdata" in main
33                        //(value of 1221), stores 1221 in "mydata"
```

Figure 4.2

Example program and output for testing pointers

```
34      *yours = temp;      //value of 999 in temp stored in
35                          //"yourdata" in main; swap is complete
36      cout << "After the swap: temp = " << temp
37             << " *mine (value) = " << *mine
38                << " *yours (value) = " << *yours << endl;
39      cout << "Exiting swap function." << endl << endl;
40 }
1  START OF MAIN (OUTPUT).
2  mydata (address) = 0x073f7a3c yourdata (address) = 0x073f7a38
3  mydata = 999 yourdata = 1221
4
5  Entering swap function.
6  mine (value) = 0x073f7a3c yours (value) = 0x073f7a38
7  Before the swap: temp = 0 *mine (value) = 999 *yours (value) = 1221
8  After the swap: temp = 999 *mine (value) = 1221 *yours (value) = 999
9  Exiting swap function.
10
11 mydata = 1221 yourdata = 999
12 END OF MAIN (OUTPUT).
```

Figure 4.2 (Continued)

The tracing code displays the start and end of program execution in main (lines 9 and 17), the entering and exiting of the swap function (lines 24 and 39), and the pointer values of mine (which has the address of mydata, lines 10–11 in main) and yours (which has the address of yourdata, lines 10–11 in main) in line 25 of the swap function. It also tracks the values of mydata and yourdata before the function call (lines12–13), just after the function call and entry into swap, but before the swap (lines 27–29), just after the swap (lines 36–38), and after returning to main (lines 15–16).

In this example the pointers do not change their original values (addresses of int variables), but in any C++ program they could be changed in any one of several ways:

```
int* newPointer;
newPointer = NULL;          //newPointer set to NULL (no address)
newPointer = mypointer;     //newPointer set to the current value of
                            //mypointer
newPointer = &yourdata;     //newPointer set to the address of the int
                            //yourdata
newPointer = new int;       //newPointer set to point to a newly
                            //allocated integer variable
                            //with no name (dynamic allocation)
```

Any of these updates to a pointer value can be traced using a cout statement before and after the update. Note that the actual addresses in the example in Fig. 4.2 (output lines 2 and 6) are shown with very strange values (a mixture of letters and numbers) due to the special format used to accommodate many millions of addresses. The actual format of the addresses is not as important as the values of the addresses. For instance in the example, the address of int my-data is shown as 0x073f7a3c and the value of the pointer mine is also shown as 0x073f7a3c. Therefore, we know that the pointer mine in the swap function contains the address of mydata in main, which is what it is supposed to do and hence our trace verifies that the program is working correctly. Pointers that have been set incorrectly should be quickly detected by the trace display so corrective action can be taken.

4.3.1 A Common Error in Using Pointers

A common error that occurs in the use of pointers is when the programmer attempts to access a dynamic variable which no longer exists. Consider the following program:

```
#include <iostream>
using namespace std;
int main ()
{
    int* mypointer;
    mypointer = new int;    // allocate space for a dynamic int variable
    *mypointer = 100;       // set that variable equal to 100
    cout << mypointer << endl << *mypointer << endl; // prints out values
    delete mypointer;       // deallocates the memory space reserved for
                            // *mypointer, but does not change the value
                            // of mypointer itself
    cout << mypointer << endl << *mypointer << endl; // ERROR
    cout << endl << "finished" << endl;      // this line may never
                                             // execute
    return 0;
}
```

When this program is run, the first output line will print values for mypointer and *mypointer as we would expect from the previous discussion. The second output line causes an error to occur. The problem is that while mypointer still contains the same address it contained earlier, the dynamic variable we created no longer exists.

Note that this error can present itself in different ways on different platforms, and even on the same platform differently on different runs. On some systems, the program may halt (a runtime error) and you may see a printed error message such as "Bus Error" or "Segmentation Fault." On other systems, there may be no error message, and the computer may even just hang, or the program may run to completion, and you may see a very odd value printed out for *mypointer by the second output line. The essence of this error is that the program has tried to access a memory location that it is not allowed to access.

4.4 STRUCTS

An *array* is a collection of data with the same data type and meaning, but with different values. A *struct* is like a database record with a collection of data of different data types and meanings, as well as different values. In a database (e.g., a personnel database) each person has a record. The record contains fields representing the attributes of each person, such as last name, first name, middle initial, address, phone, student identification number, etc. A struct has "members" which are the variables that make up the whole struct. The members of a struct are equivalent to the fields of a database record. Structs can also be declared as arrays, with each element of the array being a single struct (or record) with all its members.

Debugging programs with structs can make use of tracing by simply displaying the values of a struct's members before and after a change is made to the struct. If we are dealing with an array of structs, then individual structs (or elements) of the array can be displayed before and after changes are made to them; or, if there are many changes in the array, the entire array can be displayed.

In Fig. 4.3 we see a simple program involving a 100-element struct array for regional gas station data. Each struct has five members that hold, respectively, the station identification number, the week, the gas type, the gas price, and the gallons sold that week. The program shows how the first two records (first two elements in the struct array) might be initialized (lines 27–43), and we assume the data for the other 98 records has been read in from external files (line 45). The program then computes the total sales of gas for each type of gas from all the gas stations in the region (lines 50–64). Finally, the program displays the individual data values for each record (lines 65–66).

```
/*Debugging Example This program illustrates the use of tracing to dis-
play changes in structs during the execution of the program. */
1 #include <iostream>
2 #include <iomanip>
3 #include <string>
4 using namespace std;
5
6 const int MAX_NO_RECORDS = 100; //global constant for array of
                                  //structs
7
8 struct GasStation     //GasStation is the struct data type name
9 {
10   int station_id;
11   int week;
12   string gas_type;
13   float gas_price;
```

Figure 4.3

Example program for testing structs

```
14  float gallons_sold;
15  };
16
17  void PrintRecord (int, GasStation); //function prototype to
                                        //display one struct
18  void PrintRecords (const GasStation[]);   //function prototype
                                              //to display struct array
19
20  int main()
21  {
22      double sales_regular = 0.;
23      double sales_supreme = 0.;
24      double sales_diesel = 0.;
25      int i;
26
27      GasStation my_station[MAX_NO_RECORDS];
28
29      // initialization of first my_station record
30      my_station[0].station_id = 1;
31      my_station[0].week = 1;
32      my_station[0].gas_type = "Regular";
33      my_station[0].gas_price = 165.9;
34      my_station[0].gallons_sold = 5216.3;
35
36  //trace to display the first my_station record
37  PrintRecord (1, my_station[0]);
38
39  //initialization of second my_station record using struct
        //assignment and changes
40  my_station[1] = my_station[0];
41  my_station[1].week = 2;
42  my_station[1].gas_price = 167.9;
43  my_station[1].gallons_sold = 7311.9;
44
45  //code to read in data for the other 98 records would be
        //inserted here
46
47  //trace to display the second my_station record
48  PrintRecord (2, my_station[1]);
49
50  //To get the total sales for each type of gas, you might
        //write the following code:
51  for (i = 0; i < MAX_NO_RECORDS; i++)
52  {
```

Figure 4.3 (Continued)

```
53          if (my_station[i].gas_type == "Regular")
54              sales_regular = sales_regular +
55              my_station[i].gas_price*my_station[i].gallons_sold;
56          else if (my_station[i].gas_type == "Supreme")
57              sales_supreme = sales_supreme +
58              my_station[i].gas_price*my_station[i].gallons_sold;
59          else if (my_station[i].gas_type == "Diesel")
60              sales_diesel = sales_diesel +
61              my_station[i].gas_price*my_station[i].gallons_sold;
62          else
63              cout << "Error - wrong type of gas in array element: "
64                  << i;
65      }
66      cout << "Total Regular gas sales in the region = $" << fixed
67          << setprecision(2)
68          << sales_regular/100 << endl << endl;
69
70      // display all my_station records
71      PrintRecords (my_station);
72      return 0;
73  }
74
75  void PrintRecord (int loc, GasStation this_station)
76  {
77
78      cout << "GAS STATION STATISTICS - Location No. " << loc
79          << endl;
80      cout << " station_id week gas_type gas_price gallons_sold"
81          << endl;
82      cout << "this_station" << setw(4) << this_station.station_id
83          << setw(8) << this_station.week << setw(12)
84          << this_station.gas_type
85          << setw(10) << this_station.gas_price << setw(14)
86          << this_station.gallons_sold << endl << endl;
87  }
88
89  void PrintRecords (const GasStation my_station[])
90  {
91      int i;
92      cout << "STATISTICS FROM EACH GAS STATION IN THE REGION" << endl;
93      cout << " station_id week gas_type gas_price gallons_sold" << endl;
94      for (i = 0; i < MAX_NO_RECORDS; i++)
95      {
96          cout << "my_station[" << i << "]" << setw(4)
97              << my_station[i].station_id
```

Figure 4.3 (Continued)

```
97                  << setw(8) << my_station[i].week << setw(12)
                    << my_station[i].gas_type
98                  << setw(10) << my_station[i].gas_price << setw(14)
99                  << my_station[i].gallons_sold << endl;
100  }
101 }
```

Figure 4.3 (Continued)

The tracing code to help verify the program computations is shown in boldface. The function prototype void PrintRecord appears in line 17 for the display of a single struct (all its members), and the function itself appears in lines 75–87. The calls to the trace function PrintRecord are shown in the code (lines 36–37 and 47–48) just after the first record is initialized and again just after the second record is initialized. The output for these two traces is shown in lines 1–7 in Fig. 4.4.

Fig. 4.4 shows the trace statement output, followed by the computation of the total Regular gas sales in the region (line 9) and a partial display of the entire struct array as part of the normal output of the program (lines 11–21).


```
1   GAS STATION STATISTICS — Location No. 1
2      station_id week gas_type gas_price gallons_sold
3            1    1    Regular    165.9      5216.3
4
5   GAS STATION STATISTICS — Location No. 2
6      station_id week gas_type gas_price gallons_sold
7            1    2    Regular    167.9      7311.9
8
9   Total Regular gas sales in the region = $20930.52
10
11  STATISTICS FROM EACH GAS STATION IN THE REGION
12         station_id  week  gas_type      gas_price   gallons_sold
13  my_station[0]   1   1    Regular         165.9        5216.3
14  my_station[1]   1   2    Regular         167.9        7311.9
15  my_station[2]   1   1    Supreme         175.9         514.5
16  my_station[3]   1   2    Supreme         178.9         489.0
17  my_station[4]   2   1    Regular         160.9        4009.4
18  my_station[5]   2   2    Regular         163.9        3897.2
19  my_station[6]   2   1    Supreme         170.9         676.7
20  .........
21  my_station[99] 21   5    Diesel         1323.9        1265.4
```

Figure 4.4

Partial output from the example program to test structs

4.5 CLASSES

Classes in C++ are the basic construct for object-oriented programming. In this section we illustrate with a simple class definition GasStation the use of tracing to verify the correctness of intermediate results from a computation involving classes. In the program shown in Figure 4.5, we use the same gas station example that we used for structs in Sec. 4.4, except that GasStation is now a class consisting of arrays for each member to represent the different records in the database to keep track of gas sales. In this case, we restrict ourselves to two records for purposes of illustration, and we use tracing for all the display of record values from the GasStation objects (lines 18 for the prototype and 48 for the function call, and 52–61 for the public print function of GasStation). The tracing code and output are again shown in boldface type.

```
1 #include <iostream>
2 #include <iomanip>
3 #include <string>
4 using namespace std;
5
6 const int MAX_NO_RECS = 2; //global constant for the size of arrays
                             //in class GasStation
7
8 class GasStation
9 {
10      public:
11              int station_id[MAX_NO_RECS];
12              int week[MAX_NO_RECS];
13              string gas_type[MAX_NO_RECS];
14              float gas_price[MAX_NO_RECS];
15              float gallons_sold[MAX_NO_RECS];
16
17              void InitializeRecords();        //prototype to initialize
                                                 //an object (record)
18              void PrintRecord(int, int);      //trace prototype to
                                                 //display one record
19              void PrintRecords(int);          //prototype to display
                                                 //all objects
20              double ComputeSales();           //prototype to compute
                                                 //total gas sales
21
22 };
23
24 int main()
25 {
```

Figure 4.5

Example program for testing simple classes

```
26      double sales_regular = 0.;
27      GasStation my_station;           //create new gas station object
28
29      my_station.InitializeRecords();      // initialization
                                             // of gas station object
30      sales_regular = my_station.ComputeSales();  //get the total
                                                    //sales for Regular
gas
31      cout << "Total Regular gas sales in the region = $" << fixed
32          << setprecision(2)
33          << sales_regular << endl << endl;
34      //display all my_station records          .
35      my_station.PrintRecords(2);
36      return 0;
37  }
38
39  void GasStation::InitializeRecords()
40  {
41      int i;
42      for (i = 0; i < MAX_NO_RECS; i++)
43      {
44          cout << "Please input gas station parameters - id, week,"
45              << "gas type, price, gallons sold: "
46              << endl;
47          cin >> station_id[i] >> week[i] >> gas_type[i]
48              >> gas_price[i] >> gallons_sold[i];
49
50          //trace to display the gas station object
51          PrintRecord(i,1);
52      }
53  }
54  //Trace function for a single GasStation record
55  void GasStation::PrintRecord(int i, int loc)
56  {
57
58      cout << endl << "GAS STATION STATISTICS - Location No. "
59          << loc << endl;
60      cout << " station_id week gas_type gas_price gallons_sold"
61          << endl;
62      cout << "this_station" << setw(5) << station_id[i] << setw(8)
63          << week[i]
64          << setw(12)
65          << gas_type[i] << setw(10) << gas_price[i] << setw(14)
66          << gallons_sold[i
67          << endl << endl;
68  }
```

Figure 4.5 (Continued)

```
69
70 void GasStation::PrintRecords(int loc)
71 {
72     int i;
73     cout << "STATISTICS FROM EACH GAS STATION - Location No. "
74          << loc << endl;
75     cout << " station_id week gas_type gas_price gallons_sold"
76          << endl;
77
78     for (i = 0; i < MAX_NO_RECS; i++)
79     {
80         cout << "my_station[" << i << "]" << setw(4)
81              << station_id[i]
82              << setw(8) << week[i] << setw(12) << gas_type[i]
83              << setw(10)
84              << gas_price[i] << setw(14) << gallons_sold[i] << endl;
85     }
86 }
87
88 double GasStation::ComputeSales()
89 {
90     int i;
91     double sales_regular = 0.;
92
93     for (i = 0; i < MAX_NO_RECS; i++)
94     {
95         if (gas_type[i] == "Regular")
96         sales_regular = sales_regular +
97         gas_price[i]*gallons_sold[i];
98     }
99
100     return sales_regular/100;
101 }
```

Figure 4.5 Continued

The output from execution of the sample program in Fig. 4.5 is shown in Fig. 4.6. The normal output shows the computation of total sales of Regular gas, and the rest is trace output (in boldface type). Note that the tracing includes the location number of the trace so code and output can be easily connected.

```
Please input gas station parameters - id, week, gas type, price, gal-
lons sold:
1 1 Regular 165.9 5216.3
GAS STATION STATISTICS - Location No. 1
    station_id   week   gas_type   gas_price   gallons_sold
this_station 1    1     Regular    165.9       5216.3
Please input gas station parameters - id, week, gas type, price,
gallons sold:
1 2 Regular 167.9 7311.9
GAS STATION STATISTICS - Location No. 1
    station_id   week   gas_type   gas_price   gallons_sold
this_station 1    2     Regular    167.9       7311.9
Total Regular gas sales in the region = $20930.52
STATISTICS FROM EACH GAS STATION - Location No. 2
    station_id   week   gas_type   gas_price   gallons_sold
my_station[0] 1   1     Regular    165.9       5216.3
my_station[1] 1   2     Regular    167.9       7311.9
```

Figure 4.6

Output from the example program to test classes

This completes our discussion of the use of tracing to debug the more common C++ constructs. In the next chapter we focus on using the interactive debugger, an even more powerful tool.

CHAPTER 5

Using an Interactive Debugger

5.1 CHAPTER OBJECTIVES

- To be able to identify the fundamental commands and tools provided in modern interactive debuggers
- To be able to apply these tools to the debugging and testing of a simple C++ program
- To carefully study an example of an interactive debugging task using the Metrowerks CodeWarrior and Microsoft Visual C++ compilers

5.2 FUNDAMENTALS

In Chapters 3 and 4, you learned how to find and correct program bugs by tracing your program's behavior using extra printing statements. In this chapter, you will learn to use an additional tool, the *interactive debugger*. Note that these two tools can be used either separately or together in your work. They share the fundamental goals of pinpointing the locations where program errors occur and discovering what the errors are, while, of course, helping you correct those errors.

An interactive debugger allows you to examine the behavior of your C++ program while it is running. A debugger can be an invaluable aid in correcting errors in your code. This chapter will describe common tools available in typical modern interactive debugging systems.

The essential idea behind interactive debugging is to discover *critical points* in your program where errors occur. To do this, you can stop execution at various statements in the program and look at the values of *critical variables*. While the run is suspended, you are able to look at a *snapshot* of your program's activity. Execution then can be resumed at the point at which the program run was stopped. In addition, you may observe the program's execution in order to check its *flow of control*.

When you check the values of *critical variables*—those you believe to be important in causing your program's problems—the debugger will tell you what values the variables *actually* hold. (Note: this may not be the same as what you *want* them to hold or *think* they should hold.) If the value of some variable is not what you expected, search for the reasons for the incorrect value. Was it read improperly, or calculated improperly, or not passed back from a subprogram correctly, or something else?

The *flow of control* in a program is the order in which the program's statements are executed. You can observe this flow by running the program under the control of the debugger, which is capable both of executing one statement at a time and of executing groups of statements all at once. At all points the debugger displays a pointer to the statement which is to be executed next. Is the flow of control what you think it should be? Look for dangling `elses`, missing or out-of-order subprogram calls, infinite loops and other errors.

We recommend that you refer back to section 3.7 for the checklist that helps you identify critical variables and important locations in your program's flow of control.

In a typical modern Integrated Development Environment (IDE), you will find that the language compiler is one part of the system, and that the interactive debugger is another part. To debug your program using the debugger, you must specifically *run* the interactive debugger, which is itself a program. Then, you can run the C++ program you are working on by choosing the appropriate command from within the debugging program's menus. In this situation, you are running your C++ program under the control of the interactive debugger. Hence, the debugger allows you to observe the behavior of your C++ program as it runs.

In this discussion, we will assume that your debugger provides a typical graphical user interface (GUI), using windows and various graphical items to display information for you. Note that if you are using a text-based debugger (such as dbx on a UNIX machine), you will still find that the debugging commands and tasks described in this chapter and illustrated with examples using graphics-based debuggers are applicable to your work with a text-based debugger. This is because all debuggers provide essentially the same capabilities, whether graphics based or text based.

In sections 5.3 through 5.6, we study the use of interactive debugging techniques to debug a small example program. General debugging tools are discussed throughout the chapter. In sections 5.3 and 5.4, we specifically study the use of the Metrowerks CodeWarrior Professional Release 5 interactive debugger. In sections 5.5 and 5.6, we study the same tasks using the Microsoft

Visual C++ 6 interactive debugger. We recommend that you read the sections corresponding to the compiler you are using. If you are using another compiler, it still may be helpful you to read one of these sections because modern IDEs are all very similar.

5.3   DEBUGGING WITH METROWERKS CODEWARRIOR

5.3.1   Initiating the Debugging Process

The first step in the debugging process is usually to run or activate the interactive debugger by choosing the appropriate menu item in your IDE. In CodeWarrior, this means choosing Enable Debugger from the Project menu.

The second step involves actually initiating your C++ program's execution, under the control of the debugger. In CodeWarrior, you would choose Debug from the Project menu to begin this step. This command will load your program into memory so that it is ready to start executing under the debugger's control.

Graphics-based IDEs display your program and the debugging information you need in one or more windows on your screen. After you have started running your C++ program, one or more new windows typically appear. One window will display the C++ program and include an arrow which points to the next statement to be executed. We will call this window the *program window*, and we will call the arrow the *current statement indicator*. You also will see a list of variables which are defined in the currently executing portion of your program.

Figure 5.1 shows an example of Codewarrior's main debugging window.

In the list of variables, you will see the names of variables you have declared, and as the C++ program actually runs, you will see the current values of these variables displayed. A variable that has no current value is *undefined* or *uninitialized*, and you will see some random value represented in its location. The variables you see are *local* variables—that is, those declared in the currently executing function.

In addition, most systems will show a list of the currently active functions, in an order that shows the *call chain*, or order in which the calls occurred. For example, if during a run, the main function called the function `ProcessValues`, and `ProcessValues` called function `ReadOneItem`, you would see this list as the call chain:

```
main
ProcessValues
ReadOneItem
```

The call chain is also often called a *stack trace*. In CodeWarrior, we see this call chain in the upper left windowpane.

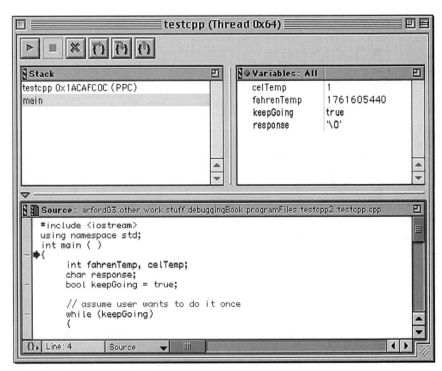

Figure 5.1

CodeWarrior's main debugging window

5.3.2 Running Your C++ Program Under Control of the Debugger

After you have activated the debugger and indicated that it must now run your program, the C++ program is stored in memory and is ready to execute under the debugger's supervision. The debugger is called *interactive* because you, the programmer, at any time can tell the debugger to display certain values or alter the flow of control of the program. The Commands that follow alter the flow of control.

Run The Run command will start actual execution of the C++ program at the first statement in the main function. If there are no breakpoints set in the program (discussed shortly), execution will continue until the program either finishes or crashes.

In CodeWarrior, you would choose Run from the Project menu to start executing the C++ program.

The Run command also is often used to *resume* execution after it has been suspended by the use of a Stop command or a breakpoint.

Stop The Stop command can be used to suspend execution of the program. Execution will be suspended at the point at which the code was executing at the time that you chose Stop.

In CodeWarrior, you would choose Stop under the Debug menu to suspend execution. The program execution will then stop, but you can restart the run from where it left off by choosing Run.

Figure 5.2 shows the Debug menu in CodeWarrior.

Kill   The Kill command will completely halt execution of your C++ program and return control to the debugger program. In CodeWarrior, Kill is found in the Control menu.

Step Commands   A Step command allows you to execute one statement. The statement that executes when you select Step is the one pointed at by the current statement indicator. After this single statement is executed, program execution will be suspended again, and you may look at variables or enter another debugging command. Using Step, you can observe the effect that one statement has on your program's behavior. Variations of step include the following:

Step Over Function Calls   Step Over allows one statement to execute, and if that one statement is a function call, the entire function will execute, leaving the current statement indicator at the statement *after* the function call. In other words, you will not see the current statement indicator move through the statements that are inside the called function.

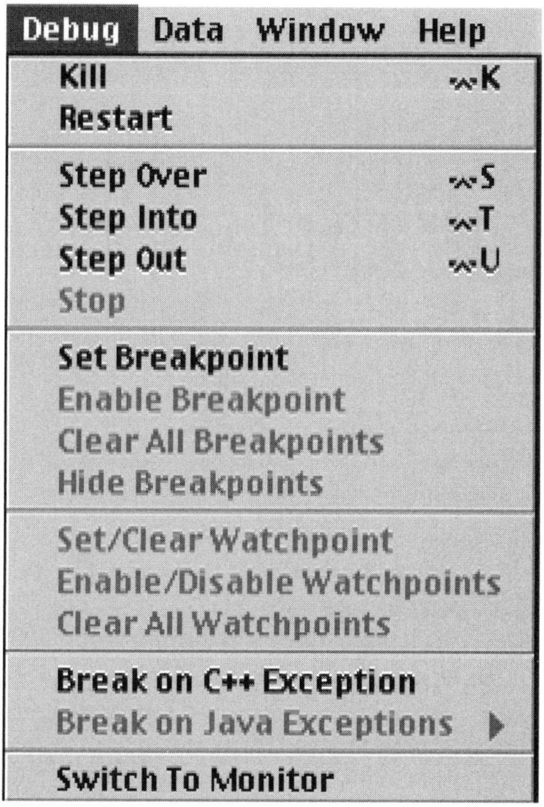

Figure 5.2

Debug menu in CodeWarrior

Step Into Function Calls　Step Into also allows one statement to execute, but if that one statement is a function call, the current statement indicator will actually enter that function. Using Step Into, you may enter a called function and then execute that function's statements one at a time.

Note that if you Step Into a standard function such as cout, you may see the actual source C++ code for cout (or sometimes its equivalent assembly language translation) in your program window. Most of the time it is preferable to Step Over standard functions rather than to enter them.

Step Out of a Function　Step Out causes the current statement indicator to exit from a function in which you currently are operating. The function will finish executing, and then you will see the current statement indicator move to the statement in the caller, just after the call to the function you just exited.

In CodeWarrior, the Step commands provided are Step Over, Step Into, and Step Out, and are found in the debugger's Debug menu.

As you execute your code using the debugger, keep in mind that your primary focus should be on examining the values of critical variables and observing the program's flow of control. The overall goal, of course, is to discover points in the program at which errors occur.

5.3.3　A Note on Infinite Loops

If your program contains an infinite loop, you can easily detect it using Step commands. As you step through the code, at some point you will see the program get stuck in a loop. In this situation the current statement arrow will keep going through the same code over and over, indefinitely. In this case, use a Kill command to completely halt the C++ program's execution.

5.3.4　Using Breakpoints

Sometimes even using the Step Over Function Calls will be too slow. You then may want to run your program at normal speed up to a certain point, then stop it and check the values of critical variables at that point. *Breakpoints* are specific statement(s) at which you want execution to be suspended.

To insert a breakpoint in your code, you typically click on the statement at which you want execution to stop, or on some indicator next to that statement. For example, in CodeWarrior, click on the gray line beside a statement. The line will become a *red* full circle, indicating that the breakpoint is *set*. Now when you run the program under the debugger's control, execution will automatically halt at this breakpoint.

You can insert as many breakpoints as you like, but only in front of executable C++ statements, not at comments, simple declarations, and so on.

To remove a breakpoint in CodeWarrior, click on the full red circle so that it becomes a flat gray line again. To remove all breakpoints simultaneously, select Clear All Breakpoints from the Debug menu.

To run a program at normal speed until a breakpoint is encountered, choose Run from the CodeWarrior debugger's Project menu. Once the program has been interrupted by a breakpoint, you can resume execution or debug using any of the commands described earlier. The Step commands may prove particularly useful once you have suspended execution at a breakpoint.

5.3.5   Changing the Value of a Variable "On the Fly"

By actually altering the value of the variable during the run, using the debugger, you can answer questions such as, "What if the variable X did have the correct value of 2.3 instead of this wrong value it now appears to have?". Your debugger probably will provide some means of doing this. In CodeWarrior, double-click on the value of the variable you want to change. Then, just type in the new value you want to use. When you resume execution, the variable will have the value you just typed in.

5.3.6   Function Pop-Up Menus

Most IDEs provide some method of easily selecting a particular function's code to display in the program window. For example, if the main function is currently displayed in the program window, but you want to look at function *MyFunc,* you can tell the debugger to bring *MyFunc* into the program window. In CodeWarrior, if you click on the { } displayed at the bottom left corner of the program window, you will see a pop-up menu of the names of the functions contained in your program, in their order of declaration. If you then select a particular function in the list, it will immediately be displayed in the program window.

5.3.7   Viewing Data Types

Data types such as `int`, `double`, etc., are usually not displayed alongside the names of variables in your debugger's windows, although most debuggers will allow you to indicate that you would like to see the data types. In CodeWarrior, to tell the debugger to show you the data types corresponding to displayed variables, choose Show Types from the Data menu.

5.3.8   Displaying Values in a Structured Type Variable

The values of structured variables such as arrays, structs, and classes typically are not all displayed in the debugger's window, unless you specifically choose to have them displayed. In CodeWarrior, to see all of the values in a structured variable, you must click on the small gray triangle pointing at that variable's name. You will see the values displayed just after the name of the variable. As an alternative, you can double-click on the variable name itself, and the values of its components will be displayed in a new window.

   Note that many debuggers, as a default, will display only the memory address of the first element in a structured variable. This can be useful debugging information as well, depending on what your program needs to do.

5.3.9   Compiler and Debugger Preferences

Most compilers allow you to alter preferences that significantly affect the behavior of the debugger. Look for a Preferences menu item to find what debugging options you have available in your local system.

For example, CodeWarrior allows you to select a preference that will cause the names of the variables that have just changed to be displayed in a highlight color of your choice.

5.4   EXAMPLE: DEBUGGING A SAMPLE C++ PROGRAM USING METROWERKS CODEWARRIOR

In this section, we will look at a short C++ program containing many bugs. Using the interactive debugger provided in Metrowerks CodeWarrior as an example, we will trace through the steps a programmer would go through in order to discover what is wrong in the program and then to fix it appropriately. The figures we show to illustrate the state of the debugger at various points were produced by CodeWarrior and are in fact "screen shots" of its debugging windows. Other modern compiler systems provide similar features.

The C++ program we will consider is intended to repeatedly read in Fahrenheit temperatures from the user, and convert each to its equivalent Celsius value. After each temperature is converted, the user is asked whether he or she would like to convert another temperature. The process is supposed to repeat until the user indicates that he or she does not want to enter any more temperature values.

5.4.1   Sample C++ Program: Version Containing Bugs

Consider the following initial version of the program, which produces no syntax errors or warnings:

```
#include <iostream>
using namespace std;
int main ( )
{
    int fahrenTemp, celTemp;
    char response;
    bool keepGoing = true;
    // assume user wants to do it once
    while (keepGoing)
    {
        // get a temp and convert it
        cout << "Enter a temperature in Fahrenheit -> ";
        cin >> fahrenTemp;
        celTemp = int(5/9 * (fahrenTemp - 32));
```

```
        cout << "In Celsius that is " << celTemp << endl;
        // ask if user wants to convert another
        cout << endl
            << "Do you want to enter another temperature?"
            << " Enter y or n -> ";
        cin >> response;
        // input error checking
        while ((response != 'y') || (response != 'n'))
        {
            cout << "Please try again. Enter y or n -> ";
            cin >> response;
        }
        // reset flag
        keepGoing = (response == 'y');
    }
    return 0;
}   // end of main
```

As we run this program, we may begin to lose patience and perhaps even our faith in computers, when we observe the following output dialogue:

```
Enter a temperature in Fahrenheit -> 75
In Celsius that is 0
Do you want to enter another temperature? Enter y or n -> y
Please try again.   Enter y or n -> y
Please try again.   Enter y or n -> y
Please try again.   Enter y or n -> y
Please try again.   Enter y or n -> n
Please try again.   Enter y or n ->
```

We finally must forcibly *quit* the program (in CodeWarrior, we use command-Q or control-Q) in order to end this misery. We then decide to use the interactive debugger to help us figure out what is wrong with the program. The next few sections illustrate this process.

5.4.2   Sample C++ Program: Using Step to Find the 1st Error

In the previous section, we saw that the calculation of the Celsius temperature produced an incorrect value of 0 for a Fahrenheit value of 75. There are two critical variables here, the first of which is `fahrenTemp`. It is possible that `fahrenTemp` is somehow not being input and stored correctly. The second critical variable is `celTemp` itself. It may not be calculated correctly. Let's check both by using the debugger to step through the program, one statement at a time, up to the point just before celTemp's value is output.

Figure 5.3 shows the CodeWarrior debugger's program window right at the point of execution of the program. In the windowpane labeled "Stack," we see the call chain. Function main is the only active function we are concerned with here. In the pane labeled "Variables," we see the four variables we have declared, celTemp, fahrenTemp, keepGoing and response. At this point the values for all of those variables are not meaningful because those variables are not initialized, containing whatever random information happens to be in their memory locations. In the pane labeled "Source" we see our C++ source program, with the current statement indicator shown as an arrow, pointing at the next statement to be executed. Note that at the beginning of the run, it points to the first brace of main.

We next use the Step Over command to execute the next few lines, bringing us to the state shown in Figure 5.4. Figure 5.4 shows the current statement indicator at the output statement for celTemp. This means that we have already entered a value for fahrenTemp, (75) and can check the variables pane to see if it is correct. We see that it is correct, so fahrenTemp is not the problem. We next look at celTemp. It is 0, which we know is wrong. So we can conclude that the assignment statement which calculates celTemp contains one or more errors.

Looking at the assignment, we notice that while the formula looks superficially correct, the value of the expression "5/9" is zero. Because we are dividing

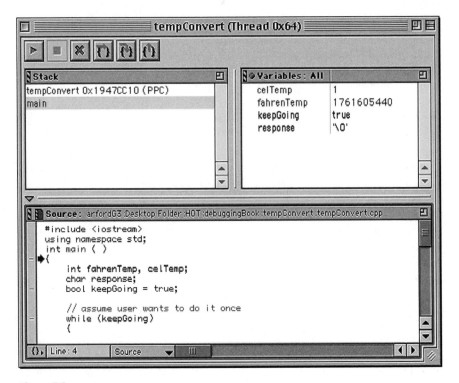

Figure 5.3

Debugging window at initial state

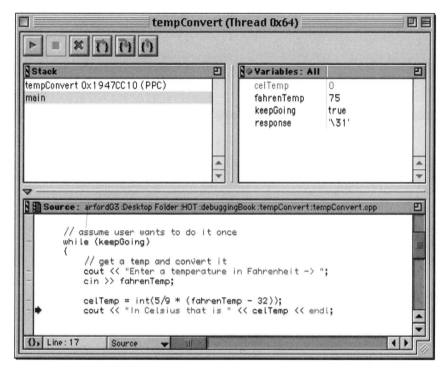

Figure 5.4

Debugging window at output line for celTemp, before correction

two integer values, any fractional portion of the result would simply be truncated. That makes the value of the entire calculation zero. If we change "5/9" to evaluate using real number division, we can fix this one problem and see if we then get a correct result.

Using the Kill command, we stop execution, go back into our program code, and change the assignment statement to read "5.0/9.0" instead of "5/9." Then, we start running the program again with Run, and use Step Over to get to the same location.

Figure 5.5 shows that we have solved our first problem. The value of cel-Temp is now 23, which is correct. We decide to Kill the program run and celebrate this small victory. Of course, the program must be tested with other temperature values before we know it is running correctly for all possible values.

5.4.3   Sample C++ Program: Using Breakpoints to Find the 2nd Error

We can guess from our original program output that we are stuck in an *infinite loop*, the loop in which we enter a *y* or an *n* to indicate whether we want to enter another temperature or not. There is one critical variable here, response.

We will set breakpoints at positions that will help us determine exactly what the problem is with this loop. There are two possible reasons the loop

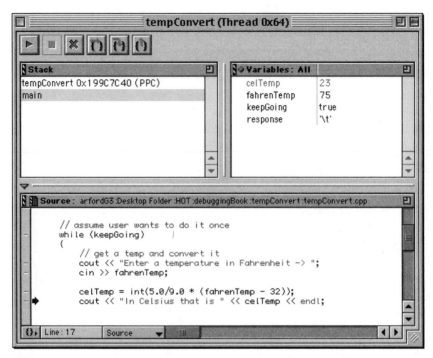

Figure 5.5

Debugging window at output line for celTemp, after correction

might be infinite: (1) The response is not read and stored correctly, or (2) the logical expression at the loop entrance is faulty, so that even if response is read and stored correctly, we remain stuck.

Figure 5.6 shows the CodeWarrior debugger's program window just at the point where we have initiated execution of the program and chosen two breakpoints. To create a breakpoint in CodeWarrior, we click on the flattened line next to a C++ statement. The flattened line then turns into a red "stop" sign, indicating a breakpoint has been set. Remember, execution will then stop just before the breakpoint statement executes.

We now start the program using Run, and it stops when it hits the first breakpoint, which is just before the loop we are concerned about. Figure 5.7 shows the state of the program when we have encountered this breakpoint and then have used Step Over to find out what will happen next. Assume that we entered a *y* when asked for a response.

Looking at the variables window, we see that response is actually *y*, which in this case, is correct. This means response is being read and stored correctly. The critical variable is fine, and the loop body should not execute at all. However, the current statement indicator shows that the next statement to be executed is the cout call, which is inside the loop and which prints a prompt for a new value. Note that if we had correctly entered an *n*, the exact same thing would have happened, indicating that we are indeed stuck in a loop. No matter

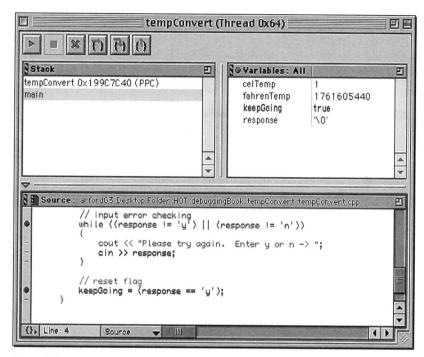

Figure 5.6

Debugging window after choosing two breakpoints

what value we type in, we remain in the loop. We can also change the value of response "on the fly" (described earlier in this chapter) to whatever value we want to check. We note that if we tried repeatedly entering values for response, we would see that the current statement indicator would never reach the 2nd breakpoint that we set. The flow of control simply cannot get to that point in the program.

So, how shall we proceed? The only possibility left is that the logical expression controlling the loop is wrong. Indeed, you may recall from Chapter 2 that the expression

```
(response != 'y')  ||  (response != 'n')
```

is always true, regardless of the value of response. This is why the loop can never exit. Realizing this, we can Kill the program, change the expression to the correct version,

```
(response != 'y')  &&  (response != 'n')
```

and run the program again. After this change, the program works correctly!

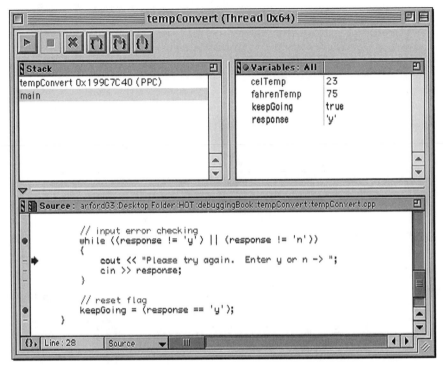

Figure 5.7

Debugging window after first breakpoint

Figure 5.8 shows that once the logical expression has been corrected, the flow of control does indeed proceed to the 2nd breakpoint we have set, where the variable keepGoing is assigned a value. Now we may stop at this point and verify that keepGoing is being set correctly. We have exited the infinite loop and successfully corrected the program.

5.4.4 Sample C++ Program: Corrected Version

The following shows the corrected program in its entirety:

```cpp
#include <iostream>
using namespace std;
int main ( )
{
    int fahrenTemp, celTemp;
    char response;
    bool keepGoing = true;
    // assume user wants to do it once
    while (keepGoing)
    {
        // get a temp and convert it
```

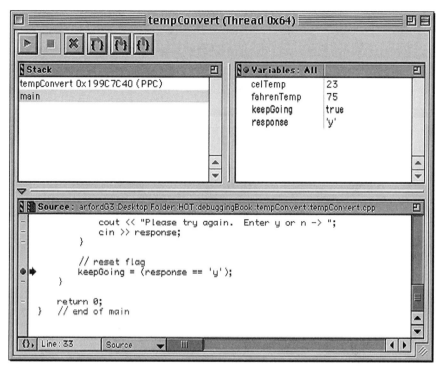

Figure 5.8

Debugging window at second breakpoint

```cpp
cout << "Enter a temperature in Fahrenheit -> ";
cin >> fahrenTemp;
celTemp = int(5.0/9.0 * (fahrenTemp - 32));
cout << "In Celsius that is " << celTemp << endl;
// ask if user wants to convert another
cout << endl
    << "Do you want to enter another temperature?"
    << " Enter y or n -> ";
cin >> response;
// input error checking
while ((response != 'y') && (response != 'n'))
{
    cout << "Please try again. Enter y or n -> ";
    cin >> response;
}
// reset flag
keepGoing = (response == 'y');
}
return 0;
} // end of main
```

When we run this version of the program, correct output is displayed as follows:

```
Enter a temperature in Fahrenheit -> 75
In Celsius that is 23
Do you want to enter another temperature? Enter y or n -> y
Enter a temperature in Fahrenheit -> 212
In Celsius that is 100
Do you want to enter another temperature? Enter y or n -> n
```

5.5   DEBUGGING WITH MICROSOFT VISUAL C++

5.5.1   Initiating the Debugging Process

The first step in the debugging process is usually to run or activate the interactive debugger by choosing the appropriate menu item in your IDE. In Visual C++, we first go to the Build menu and choose Set Active Configurations. This will cause a dialog box to appear. In this dialog box, make sure that the highlighted line ends with Win 32 Debug. If that line is not highlighted, click on it to select it, and then click OK. In this discussion, we assume you set up your project as a *Win 32 Console Application.*

The next step involves actually initiating your C++ program's execution, under the control of the debugger. In Visual C++, you would choose Start Debug from the Build menu and then choose Step Into from the submenu that immediately appears. This command will load your program into memory and start executing your main function.

Graphics-based IDEs display your program and the debugging information you need in one or more windows on your screen. After you have started running your C++ program, you will see the Visual C++ window change. We will call the new window the *debugging window.* One pane will display the C++ program. We will call this the *program pane.*

Figure 5.9 illustrates the main debugging window of Visual C++, along with its initial Start Debug menu.

Once your program is running under the debugger, the program pane will include an arrow pointing to the next statement to be executed. We will call this the *current statement indicator.* You will also see a list of variables which are defined in the currently executing portion of your program. This list of variables will appear in the lower left pane, labeled with the word *Context.* We will call this display the *variables pane.* This pane includes tabs to select various types of variables, such as auto, local, etc. (Take a look at Figure 5.12 at this time to see examples of these items.)

In the list of variables, you will see the names of variables you have declared; as the C++ program actually runs, you will see the current values of these variables. If a value is red, it has just changed. A variable having no current value is *undefined* or *uninitialized,* and you will see some random value represented in its place. The variables you typically want to see are *local* variables—that is, those declared in the currently executing function.

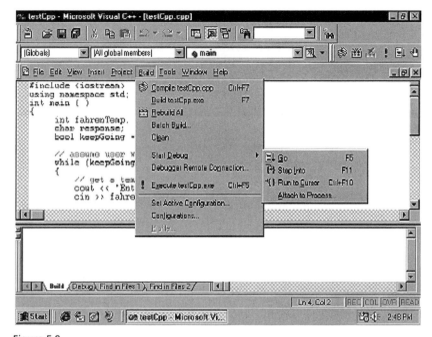

Figure 5.9

Visual C++ main debugging window and Start Debug menu

On your lower right, you will see *the watch pane*. You can drag highlighted variables or expressions to this pane to see their values displayed there.

In addition, most systems will show a list of the currently active functions, in an order which shows the *call chain*, or order in which the calls occurred. For example, if during a run, the main function called function ProcessValues, and ProcessValues called function ReadOneItem, you would see this list as the call chain:

```
main
ProcessValues
ReadOneItem
```

The call chain is also often called a *stack trace*. In Visual C++, we can look at the call chain by clicking on the triangle next to Context in the lower left pane.

5.5.2   Running Your C++ Program Under Control of the Debugger

After you have activated the debugger and indicated that it must now run your program, the C++ program is stored in memory and is ready to execute under the debugger's supervision. The debugger is called *interactive* because you, the programmer, at any time can tell the debugger to display certain values or alter the flow of control of the program. Commands that alter the flow of control are found in the Debug menu and in the corresponding Debug toolbar which appears when debugging.

Figure 5.10 shows you the Visual C++ Debug menu.

Figure 5.11 displays the corresponding Debug toolbar, which contains most of the same commands, but in button form.

The commands that follow are debugging commands.

Go   The Go command will start actual execution of your C++ program, at the first statement in the main function. If there are no breakpoints set in the program (discussed later), execution will continue until the program either finishes or crashes.

The Go command is also used to resume execution after it has been suspended—by a breakpoint, for example.

Restart   The Restart command is used to reintialize your debugging session, (i.e., start over).

Run to Cursor   The Run to Cursor command can be used to execute all statements up to a particular program statement. Place the cursor on a line in the program below the line currently active. Then choose Run to Cursor.

Stop Debugging   The Stop Debugging command will completely halt execution of your C++ program and return control to Visual C++.

Step Commands   A Step command allows you to execute one statement. The statement that executes when you select Step is the one pointed at by the current statement indicator. After this single statement is executed, program execution will be suspended again and you may look at variables or enter another debugging command. Using Step, you can observe the effect that one statement has on your program's behavior. Variations of step include the following:

Step Over Function Calls   Step Over allows one statement to execute, and if that one statement is a function call, the entire function will execute, leaving the current statement indicator at the statement *after* the function call. In other words, you will not see the current statement indicator move through the statements which are inside the called function.

Step Into Function Calls   Step Into also allows one statement to execute, but if that one statement is a function call, the current statement indicator will actually enter that function. Using Step Into, you may enter a called function and then execute that function's statements one at a time.

Note that if you Step Into a standard function such as cout, you may see the actual source C++ code for cout, or sometimes its equivalent assembly language translation, in your program window. Most of the time it is preferable to Step Over standard functions rather than to enter them.

Step Out of a Function   Step Out causes the current statement indicator to exit from a function in which you currently are operating. The function will

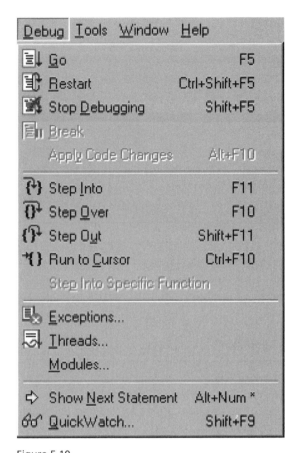

Figure 5.10

Figure 5.10 Visual C++ Debug menu

Figure 5.11

Visual C++ Debug toolbar

finish executing, and then you will see the current statement indicator move to the statement in the caller, just after the call to the function you just exited.

As you execute your code using the debugger, keep in mind that your primary focus should be on examining the values of critical variables and observing the program's flow of control. The overall goal, of course, is to discover points in the program where errors occur.

5.5.3   A Note on Infinite Loops

If your program contains an infinite loop, you can easily detect it using Step commands. As you step through the code, at some point you will see the program get "stuck" inside some loop. In this situation the current statement arrow will just keep going through the same code over, and over. In this case, click on the X in the upper-right corner of your program's output window to completely halt the C++ program's execution.

5.5.4   Using Breakpoints

Sometimes even stepping with Step Over Function Calls will be too slow. You may want to run your program at normal speed up to a certain point, then stop it and check the values of critical variables at that point. *Breakpoints* are specific statement(s) at which you want your program execution to be suspended.

To the left of the main program editing window is a grey column. In this column, right click to the left of any statement in your program, and a menu will appear. Choose Insert/Remove Breakpoint from this menu. Now a small red octagon, like a stop sign, will appear next to the program line. This indicates that a breakpoint has been *set* at that statement. When you run the program now under the debugger's control, execution will automatically halt at this breakpoint.

You can insert as many breakpoints as you wish, but only in front of executable C++ statements, not at comments, simple declarations, and so on.

To remove a breakpoint in Visual C++, right click on the red octagon to obtain the menu again. Choose Remove Breakpoint. To remove all breakpoints in a program simultaneously, select Breakpoints from the Edit menu. Then click on Remove All.

To run a program at normal speed until a breakpoint is encountered, choose Go from the Visual C++ debugger's Debug menu. Once the program has been interrupted by a breakpoint, you can resume execution or debug using any of the commands described earlier. The Step commands may prove particularly useful once you have suspended execution at a breakpoint.

5.5.5   Changing the Value of a Variable "On the Fly"

As with CodeWarrior, in Visual C++ you also can answer questions such as, "What if the variable X did have the correct value of 2.3 instead of this wrong value it now has?" Again, this is accomplished by actually altering the value of the variable during the run, using the debugger. The debugger usually provides some means of doing this. In Visual C++, just double-click on the value of the variable you want to change in the variables pane. Then, type in the new value you want to use, and hit the Enter key. When you resume execution, the variable will have the value you just typed in.

5.5.6 Function Pop-Up Menus

Most IDEs provide some method of easily selecting a particular function's code to display in the program pane. For example, if the main function is currently displayed in the program window, but you want to look at function MyFunc, you can tell the debugger to bring MyFunc into the program window. In Visual C++, if you click on the small triangle displayed next to the word *main* shown above the program pane, you will see a pop-up menu of the names of the functions contained in your program, in their order of declaration. If you then select a particular function in the list, it will immediately be displayed in the program window.

5.5.7 Viewing Data Types

Data types (such as int, double, etc.) are usually not displayed alongside the names of variables in your debugger's windows; most debuggers will, however, allow you to indicate that you would like to see data types. In Visual C++, to tell the debugger to show you the data type which corresponds to a particular variable, right click on the variable name in the variables pane, and then select Properties.

5.5.8 Displaying Values in a Structured Type Variable

The values of structured variables such as arrays, structs, and classes are typically not all displayed in the debugger's window, unless you specifically choose to have them displayed. In Visual C++, to see all of the values in a structured variable, you must click on the '+' to the left of that variable's name in the variables pane.

Note that many debuggers, as a default, will display only the memory address of the first element in a structured variable. This can be useful debugging information as well, depending on what your program needs to do.

5.5.9 Compiler and Debugger Preferences

Most compilers allow you to alter preferences which significantly affect the behavior of the debugger. In Visual C++, go to Options under the Tools menu to set your preferences.

5.6 EXAMPLE: DEBUGGING A SAMPLE C++ PROGRAM USING MICROSOFT VISUAL C++

In this section, we will look at a short, buggy C++ program. Using the interactive debugger provided in Visual C++ as an example, we will trace through the steps a programmer would go through in order to discover what is wrong in the program and then to fix it appropriately. The figures we show to illustrate the state of the debugger at various points were produced by Visual C++ and are in fact "screen shots" of its debugging windows. Other modern compiler systems provide similar features.

As in the CodeWarrior example, here too the C++ program is intended to repeatedly read in Fahrenheit temperatures from the user, and convert each to its equivalent Celsius value. After each temperature is converted, the user is asked whether he or she would like to convert another temperature. The process is supposed to repeat until the user indicates that he or she does not want to enter any more temperature values.

5.6.1   Sample C++ Program: Buggy Version

Consider the following initial version of the program, which produces no syntax errors or warnings:

```cpp
#include <iostream>
using namespace std;
int main ( )
{
    int fahrenTemp, celTemp;
    char response;
    bool keepGoing = true;
    // assume user wants to do it once
    while (keepGoing)
    {
        // get a temp and convert it
        cout << "Enter a temperature in Fahrenheit -> ";
        cin >> fahrenTemp;
        celTemp = int(5/9 * (fahrenTemp - 32));
        cout << "In Celsius that is " << celTemp << endl;
        // ask if user wants to convert another
        cout << endl
            << "Do you want to enter another temperature?"
            << " Enter y or n -> ";
        cin >> response;
        // input error checking
        while ((response != 'y') || (response != 'n'))
        {
            cout << "Please try again. Enter y or n -> ";
            cin >> response;
        }
        // reset flag
        keepGoing = (response == 'y');
    }
    return 0;
}  // end of main
```

When we run this program and observe the following output dialogue, we may begin to question our programming skills or perhaps our sanity.

```
Enter a temperature in Fahrenheit -> 75
In Celsius that is 0
Do you want to enter another temperature? Enter y or n -> y
Please try again.   Enter y or n -> y
Please try again.   Enter y or n -> y
Please try again.   Enter y or n -> y
Please try again.   Enter y or n -> n
Please try again.   Enter y or n ->
```

We have to forcibly quit the program (in Visual C++, we click on the X in the upper right corner of the program's output window) in order to end this loop. We then decide to use the interactive debugger to help us figure out what's wrong. The next few sections illustrate this process.

5.6.2   Sample C++ Program: Using Step to Find the 1st Error

We see that the calculation of the Celsius temperature produces an incorrect value of 0 for a Fahrenheit value of 75. There are two critical variables here, first, fahrenTemp. It is possible that fahrenTemp is somehow not being input and stored correctly. The second critical variable is celTemp itself which may not be calculated correctly. Let's check both by using the debugger to step through the program, one statement at a time, up to the point just before celTemp's value is output.

Figure 5.12 shows the Visual C++ debugging window at a point just after we initiated execution of the program using Step Into and then used Step Over to complete the variable declarations. In the variables pane, we see the four variables we have declared, celTemp, fahrenTemp, keepGoing and response. At this point the values for all but keepGoing are not meaningful, because those variables are not initialized and thus contain whatever random information happens to be in their memory locations. In the program pane we see our C++ source program, with the current statement indicator shown as an arrow, pointing at the next statement to be executed.

We next use the Step Over command to execute the next few lines, bringing us to the state shown in Figure 5.13. Figure 5.13 shows the current statement indicator at the output statement for celTemp. This means that we have already entered a value for fahrenTemp (75), and can check the variables pane to see if it is correct. It is correct, so fahrenTemp is not the problem. We next look at celTemp. It is 0, which we know is wrong, so we conclude that the assignment statement which calculates celTemp contains at least one error.

Note that to interactively enter an input value for fahrenTemp, at the point at which you would use Step Over to execute "cin >> fahrenTemp," you would have to click on the button at the bottom of the screen labeled testCpp, which would pull up the output window (console window) for your executing C++ program. The name of this button would correspond to the name of your program's executable file (here, testCpp.exe).

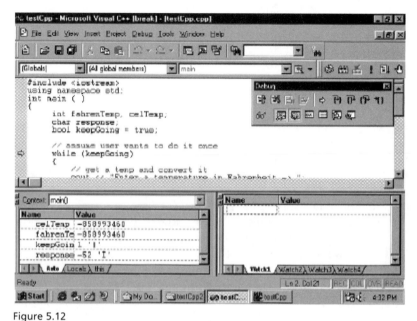

Figure 5.12

Debugging window after variable declarations completed

Looking at the assignment, we notice that while the formula looks superficially correct, the value of the expression "5/9" is zero. Because we are dividing

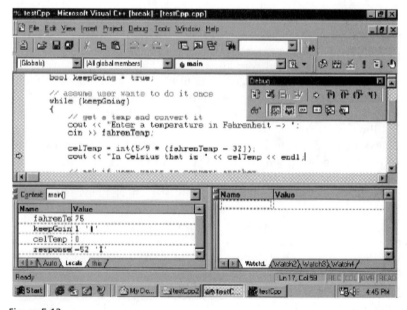

Figure 5.13

Debugging window at output line for celTemp, before correction two integer values, any fractional portion of the result would simply be truncated. That makes the value of the entire calculation zero. If we change "5/9" to evaluate using real number division, we can fix this one problem and then see if we get a correct result.

Using the Stop Debugging command, we stop execution, go back into our program code, and change the assignment statement so that it reads "5.0/9.0" instead of "5/9." Then, we start running the program again with Step Into, and use Step Over to get to the same location.

Figure 5.14 shows that we have solved our first problem. The value of celTemp is now 23, which is correct. We decide to Stop Debugging the program run and celebrate our first small victory. Of course, the program must be tested with other temperature values before we know it is running correctly for all possible values.

5.6.3   Sample C++ Program: Using Breakpoints to Find the 2nd Error

We can guess from our original program output that we are stuck in an *infinite loop*, the loop in which we enter a *y* or an *n* to indicate whether we want to enter another temperature or not. There is one critical variable here, *response*.

We will set breakpoints at positions that will help us determine exactly what the problem is with this loop. There are two possible reasons the loop might be infinite: (1) response is not read and stored correctly, or (2) the logical expression at the loop entrance is faulty, so that even if response is read and stored correctly, we remain stuck.

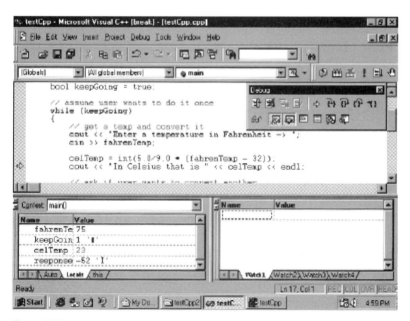

Figure 5.14

Debugging window at output line for celTemp, after correction

Figure 5.15 shows the Visual C++ debugging window just at the point where we have initiated execution of the program and chosen two break-points. Remember that execution will stop just before a breakpoint statement executes. Notice also that we have decided to keep a special eye on the value of response. By clicking on the variable name in its declaration to highlight it, then dragging it to the watch pane, we will make it a bit easier to notice any changes in its value.

We now run the program using Go, and it stops when it hits the first breakpoint, just prior to the `while` loop we are concerned about. Figure 5.16 shows the state of the program when we have encountered this breakpoint and then used Step Over to find out what happens next. Assume we entered a 'y' when asked for a response.

Looking at the watch pane, we see that response is actually *y*, which in this case, is correct. This means response is being read and stored correctly. The critical variable is fine, and the loop body should not execute at all. However, the current statement indicator shows that the next statement to be executed is the `cout` call inside the loop, which prints a prompt for a new value. Note that if we had correctly entered an *n*, the exact same thing would have happened. We are indeed stuck in this loop. No matter what value we type in, we remain in the loop. We can also change the value of response "on the fly" (described earlier in

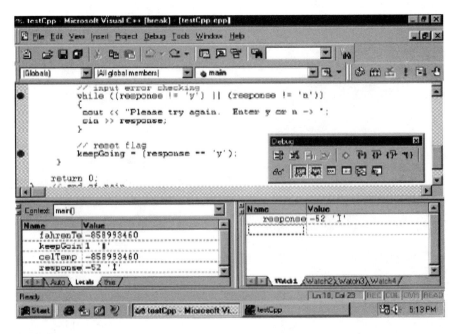

Figure 5.15

Debugging window after choosing two breakpoints

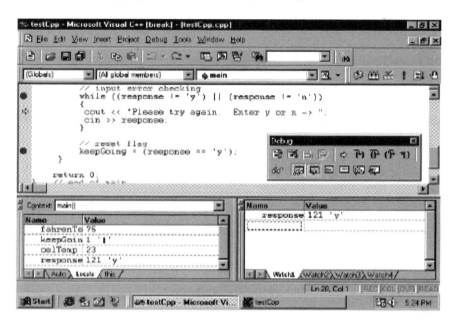

Figure 5.16

Debugging window after first breakpoint

this chapter) to whatever value we want to check that this is the case. We note that if we tried repeatedly entering values for response, we would see that the current statement indicator would never reach the 2nd breakpoint that we set. The flow of control cannot get there.

Now what? The only possibility left is that the logical expression controlling the loop is wrong. Indeed, you may recall from Chapter 2 that the expression

```
(response != 'y')  ||  (response != 'n')
```

is always true, regardless of the value of response. This is why the loop can never exit. Realizing this, we can Stop Debugging the program, change the expression to the correct version,

```
(response != 'y')  &&  (response != 'n')
```

and run the program again. After this change, the program works correctly!

Figure 5.17 shows that once the logical expression has been corrected, the flow of control does indeed proceed to the 2nd breakpoint we set, where the variable keepGoing is assigned a value. We can now stop at this point and verify that keepGoing is being set correctly if we wish. We have exited the infinite loop and successfully corrected the program.

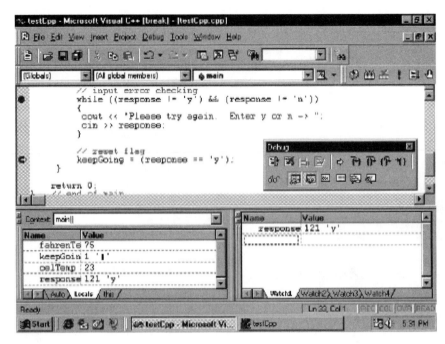

Figure 5.17

Debugging window at second breakpoint

5.6.4   Sample C++ Program: Corrected Version

Please see section 5.4.4 for the corrected program in its entirety.

APPENDIX A

The 32 Most Common Bugs in First Programs

In this appendix we summarize the 32 most common bugs found in first programs based on our experience with introductory programming classes over the past decade. This is by no means an exhaustive list, but it is given as a checklist for beginning programmers to analyze their code in advance for potential bugs. More details about how to detect and correct these bugs (errors) are given in the sections of the book shown in parentheses.

1. array as a parameter handled improperly (Sec. 2.2)
2. array index out of bounds (Sec. 3.6)
3. call-by-value used instead of call-by-reference for function parameters to be modified
4. comparison operators misused (Sec. 3.3)
5. compound statement not used (Sec. 2.4)
6. dangling else (Sec. 2.4)
7. division by zero attempted
8. division using integers, so quotient gets truncated (Sec. 3.3)
9. files not closed properly (and thus the buffers were not flushed)
10. infinite loop (Sec. 2.4)
11. global variables used – not a bug, but bad programming practice
12. if-else not used properly (Sec. 3.3)
13. left hand side of assignment does not contain an L-value (Sec. 2.2)
14. loop has no body (Sec. 2.3)

15. missing "&" or missing "const" with a call-by-reference function parameter
16. missing bracket for body of function or compound statement
17. missing reference to namespace (Sec. 2.2)
18. missing return statement in a value-returning function (Sec. 2.2)
19. missing semi-colon in simple statements, function prototypes, struct definitions, or class definitions (Sec. 2.2)
20. mismatched data types in expressions
21. operator precedence misunderstood (Sec. 2.4)
22. off-by-one error in a loop (Sec. 2.4, 3.3)
23. overused (overloaded) local variable names, leading to confusion
24. pointers not set properly or overwritten in error (Sec. 4.3)
25. return with value attempted in a void function
26. undeclared variable name (Sec. 2.2)
27. uninitialized variable (Sec. 2.3, 3.3)
28. unmatched parentheses (Sec. 2.2)
29. unterminated strings (Sec. 2.2)
30. using " = " when " ==" is intended (Sec. 2.3)
31. using "&" when "&&" is intended in an "if" or loop expression
32. "while" used improperly instead of "if" (Sec. 3.6)

Checklist for Error Detection and Prevention

The details of error (bug) detection and prevention methods have been very well covered by outstanding programmers and authors such as Brian Kernighan and Rob Pike in their book *The Practice of Programming* [KePi99]. Other good ideas have appeared recently in books by Scott Meyers [Meye92] and Steve Maguire [Magu93] based on the Microsoft experience. Our intent here is to categorize the fundamental ideas expressed by these and other experienced programmers as a checklist for the new programmer, and we hope you will read those works in depth as you progress in your programming skills.

B.1   ERROR DETECTION METHODS

Error detection methods are used to find errors that have caused the program to run incorrectly. Syntax errors will automatically be detected by your C++ compiler. Semantic errors include those that cause the program to crash or go into an infinite loop. Other semantic errors may not cause any obvious crashes or loops, but result in incorrect output. Both types of semantic errors can usually be detected with the following methods:

1. Use the tracing method described in this book (see Chaps. 3, 4) to display the value of critical variables, including arrays, vectors, strings, pointers, struct members, and class members. Display them both before and after their modification in the program. The more tracing statements you put into the program, the more you can localize the problem and target in on the real error. This is often referred to as a "divide and conquer" technique.

2. Try to make the error reproducible. This will help in locating the error if you can easily reproduce its occurrence while making small changes in your code to find the problem. Errors that are not reproducible are probably due to system or hardware errors and may not be in your code.

3. Get a stack trace of function calls to see if functions are being called in the correct sequence. This feature is usually provided as part of an interactive debugger (see Chap. 5). The debugger is a critical tool to use for error detection if simple tracing fails to find the error.

4. Once an error is found, correct it immediately while you understand what the problem is and can easily make the fix. Then check to see whether the same mistake has been made elsewhere and fix those occurrences immediately.

5. Examine the most recent code change. Very often, corrections to errors contain new errors, so it is useful to carefully check all changes just made.

B.2 ERROR PREVENTION AND TESTING METHODS

1. Use good design techniques, good programming style (use indentation, do not use global variables, etc.), and well-designed interfaces among functions and with the user [KePi99].

2. Study your code thoroughly before typing it in or before running it. This is often referred to as a code inspection or walkthrough. Explain your code to someone else if possible—ideally to another programmer you are working with—as part of the walkthrough.

3. Make your program self-documented with comments to describe the definitions of all variables, the purpose of functions and interfaces to functions, and a brief description of the purpose of each control structure (loop, selection statement, or function).

4. Insert assertions and self-checking code to test for the possibility of bad input data to the program, and protect the program from crashing with bad data. This is also referred to as *defensive programming*.

5. Test your code at the boundary values for variables and for pre- and post-conditions. This involves tracing variables used just before and after control structures are entered (selection statements "`if`" and "`switch`," looping statements "`while`", "`do while`", and "`for`," and function calls), tracing of values used inside these control structures including testing the execution of each branch in selection statements, and testing "`for`" and "`while`" loops so the loop indexes are properly set before the loop executes and when it finishes. This technique can also be used to avoid the division-by-zero problem.

6. Avoid the problem of error recurrence by keeping a log of all bugs fixed.

7. Test your program incrementally, after each function is written, or subdivide a function into parts that can be tested independently. Don't wait until you have ALL the code written before doing any testing. By then, the errors will be much harder to localize and detect.

8. Consider these behavioral properties in all programs:

    Correctness: Does the program produce correct output for correct input?

    Reliability (robustness): Does the program handle incorrect data properly?

    Utility: Is the program easy to use?

    Performance: Is the program efficient—that is, does it execute quickly enough to satisfy the needs of the user of the program?

Bibliography

[Bugg98]   Bugg, K. *Debugging C++ Windows* , R & D Books, 1998.

[DeDe01]   Deitel, H.M. and Deitel, P.J. *C++ How to Program*, 3rd Edition, Prentice Hall, 2001.

[KePi99]   Kernighan, B.W. and Pike, R. *The Practice of Programming*, Addison-Wesley, 1999.

[Lenc00]   Lencevicius, R. *Advanced Debugging Methods*, Kluwer Academic Publishing, 2000.

[Magu93]   Maguire, S. *Writing Solid Code*, Microsoft Press, 1993.

[McCo93]   McConnell, S. *Code Complete*, Microsoft Press, 1993.

[Meye92]   Meyers, S. *Effective C++*, Addison-Wesley, 1992.

[PaMu00]   Pappas, C.H. and Murray, W.H. III *Debugging C++: Troubleshooting for Programmers*, McGraw-Hill, 2000.

[Robb00]   Robbins, J. *Debugging Applications*, Microsoft Press, 2000.

[Rose00]   Rosenberg, J.B. *How Debuggers Work: Algorithms, Data Structures, and Architecture*, Wiley, 1996.

[Savi01]   Savitch, W. *Problem Solving With C++*, 3rd Edition, Addison Wesley, 2001.

[Stit92]   Stitt, M. *Debugging: Creative Techniques and Tools for Software Repair* , Wiley, 1992.

Index